The North West Way

By

Steve Garrill

TRAIL GUIDES
publications

First published in Great Britain in 2013 by Trailguides Limited.
www.trailguides.co.uk

ISBN 978-1-905444-58-8

The right of Steve Garrill to be identified as the author of this book has been asserted in accordance with the Copyright, Design and Patents Act 1988.

All rights reserved. No part of this publication may be reproduced, stored in a retrieval system, or transmitted in any form or by any means (electronic, mechanical photocopying, recording or otherwise), without the written permission of Trailguides Limited.

Copyright © 2013 Steve Garrill

The route diagrams in this book are based upon 1925-1940 Ordnance Survey One-Inch maps updated by field trips and site visits.

Trailguides Limited
35 Carmel Road South
Darlington
Co Durham DL3 8DQ

Cover design by Steve Gustard
Artwork by Trailguides Limited

CONTENTS

	Page
Introduction	
1. Introduction	4
2. Equipment	5
3. Mapping	6
4. Preston	6
5. Carlisle	8
Day 1: Preston to Hurst Green	11
Day 2: Hurst Green to Gisburn	22
Day 3: Gisburn to Malham	31
Day 4: Malham to Horton-in-Ribblesdale	40
Day 5: Horton-in-Ribblesdale to Hawes	51
Day 6: Hawes to Keld	60
Day 7: Keld to Baldersdale	69
Day 8: Baldersdale to Langdon Beck	79
Day 9: Langdon Beck to Dufton	90
Day 10: Dufton to Garrigill	100
Day 11: Garrigill to Haltwhistle	109
Day 12: Haltwhistle to Walton	119
Day 13: Walton to Carlisle	132
Appendix	
Ferguson Grading System	139
The Author	142
Trailguides Limited	143
Disclaimer	144

Cover photos.
Front cover. Maize Beck. Day 9 Langdon Beck to Dufton.
Back cover. Heading towards Pen-y-Ghent. Day 4 Malham to Horton-in-Ribblesdale.

INTRODUCTION

1. Introduction

This walk was devised to incorporate some of the best walking in the north of England. It has been broken into manageable sections with overnight stops where good accommodation is available. Starting and finishing at mainline railway stations, this walk is designed for anyone of reasonable fitness. Based on years of experience of walking using guidebooks which are vague, misleading and sometimes simply totally wrong, the author has taken great care to give simple instructions which have been rigorously checked.

Starting in Preston the walk follows the Ribble Way on the riverside paths of the delightful Ribble Valley, through Ribchester and Hurst Green to Gisburn. Shortly after Gisburn it heads eastwards to pick up the Pennine Way at Malham with its dramatic limestone outcrops. Follow it northwards through what anyone who has completed the Pennine Way would agree is its best section. There are many scenic highlights such as the exciting scramble over Pen-y-Ghent, the formidable heights of Great Dun Fell and Cross Fell, the awesome falls of High Force, the glacial valley of High Cup Nick - which many consider to be the highlight of the walk and many more too numerous to mention. At Alston, the highest market town in England, the Pennine Way reaches one of its poorer sections. Our walk instead takes a more gentle route up the beautiful South Tyne Trail, following the line of a disused railway to Haltwhistle. The walk now links with the Hadrian's Wall National Trail and heads west towards Carlisle along an inspiring walk rich with history and over the incomparable Walltown Craggs, one of the highlights of walking in the north of England.

By combining the best sections of established walks, there is the added advantage of routes which are marked on OS maps/GPS to cross-reference against the detailed instructions in this book. Apart from all the different types of walking involved, there are many interesting small museums, towns and villages with friendly people, good food and real ale available. Walking is increasingly popular in Britain, you will still find solitude, but be aware that accommodation is limited in places. If you plan to complete the walk in one go, in my opinion the best way, then start to book your accommodation many weeks in advance. I have indicated where places to stay are particularly limited.

			Miles
Day 1	Preston	Hurst Green	17
Day 2	Hurst Green	Gisburn	19
Day 3	Gisburn	Malham	18.5

Day 4	Malham	Horton	15.5
Day 5	Horton	Hawes	14
Day 6	Hawes	Keld	13
Day 7	Keld	Baldersdale	15
Day 8	Baldersdale	Langdon Beck	15.5
Day 9	Langdon Beck	Dufton	14
Day 10	Dufton	Garrigill	16
Day 11	Garrigill	Haltwhistle	18
Day 12	Haltwhistle	Walton	17.5
Day 13	Walton	Carlisle	12
			205

2. Equipment

Without a doubt the single most important item is a pair of good, waterproof boots which are well worn in. The route is rocky in places, muddy in others, and boots which are up to the job in hand are essential. My personal preference is Alt-berg (thanks to Jon from Whalley Warm & Dry for advice and fitting service) - mine have covered thousands of miles, never leaked and I have never had a blister.

I also carry a compass, lightweight LED torch, emergency whistle, water and emergency rations. I have never experienced a blister, but if you think you might, carry a blister plaster (Compeed or second skin). As a precaution carry antiseptic wipes and plasters. Mobile phones are of course very useful but you will find yourself out of signal on many sections of the walk. Always give an estimated time of arrival at your destination and contact them if you are likely to be seriously late. Leave a copy of your itinerary with your family or a friend.

Weather conditions can change quickly, and temperatures vary significantly, especially on the high fells. Have several layers rather than one thick layer and good, breathable waterproofs. You will need a rucksack which is waterproof but strongly resist the temptation to carry too much. Over the years I have reduced the amount I carry significantly, thanks largely to having become a huge fan of Rohan clothing. Their clothes are tough and functional but still look smart. Best of all they can be rinsed through and will dry completely overnight so you don't need to carry extra sets of clothing. My last piece of advice is to carry a spare pair of socks. Sit down mid-way through a hard day's walking, take your boots off and put on clean, dry socks - heavenly!

3. Mapping

Despite having rigorously checked the instructions in this book many times, I would still advise having OS maps - the necessary map is stated at the start of each section. A much better alternative to OS Maps, especially on a wet and/or windy day (inevitable!) is a decent modern GPS. There are many devices on the market. My first device, which for obvious reasons I cannot name, was pretty useless. The clear market leader is the latest Satmap Active 10 (www.satmap.co.uk), a considerable investment but well worth purchasing for a serious walker and the support from Satmap is outstanding. If you're caught up on the high fells in adverse weather conditions, tired, hungry and uncertain of your location, it will seem a small investment indeed!

Maps required:
OS Explorer 286 Blackpool & Preston.
OS Explorer 287 West Pennine Moors.
OL41 Forest of Bowland and Ribblesdale.
OL2 Yorkshire Dales Southern & Western.
OL30 Yorkshire Dales Northern and Central.
OL31 North Pennines Teesdale and Weardale.
OL19 Howgill Fells and Upper Eden Valley.
OL43 Hadrian's Wall Haltwhistle and Hexham.
OS Explorer 315 Carlisle

The route descriptions included in this book are meant as a guide and although under normal conditions they should be sufficient to guide you round the route they are not intended to replace the use of the relevant map. Nor is the sketch diagram of the route meant to replace the OS map but rather to be used as an aid for you to identify the route on the map.

This countryside can be wild and rough, which is part of its attraction, and the weather can be very changeable. It is quite possible to set off in brilliant sunshine and then to find that later, low cloud and rain has come rolling in and visibility is very poor. The ability to navigate with map and compass is a required skill to safely traverse these hills and it would be extremely foolhardy to venture out with just this guidebook and no map.

4. Preston

Preston (www.preston.gov.uk) is the administrative centre of Lancashire and became the City of Preston with a population of 132,000 in 2002. Historically it was the lowest point at which the Ribble could be bridged.

Outline of the route.

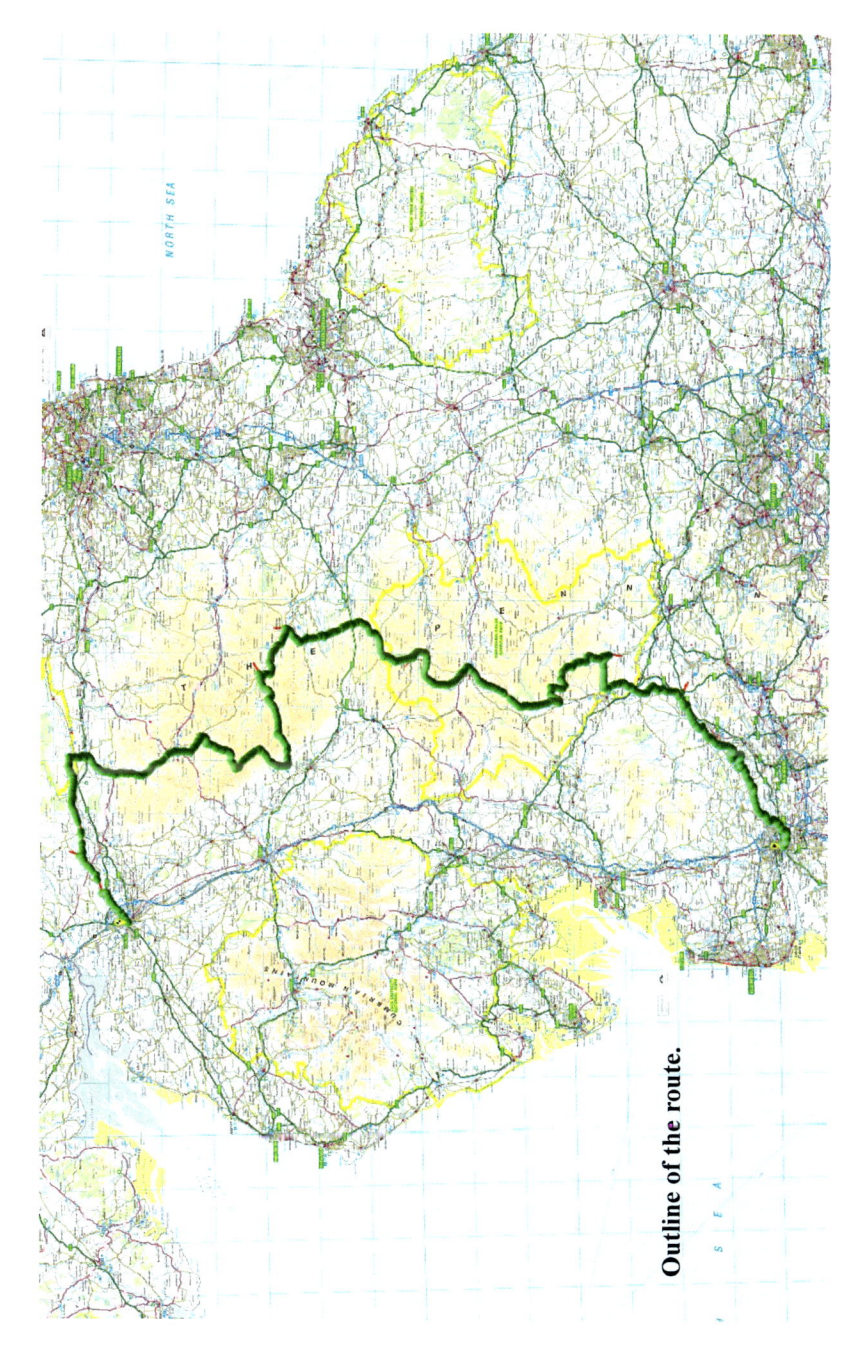

The Preston area has much evidence of ancient Roman activity in the area, especially a Roman road leading to a camp at Walton-le-Dale. Preston was established by the Saxons. The name Preston is derived from Old English words meaning "Priest settlement" and appears in the *Domesday Book* as "Prestune". During the Middle Ages Preston formed a parish and township and was granted a Guild Merchant charter in 1179, giving it the status of a market town. It was a medieval town of some importance and had a representative in parliament as early as 1295. Textiles have been produced in Preston since the middle of the 13th century, when locally produced wool was woven in people's houses. Flemish weavers settled in the area during the 14th century and helped to develop the industry. Sir Richard Arkwright, inventor of the water frame for spinning cotton, was a weaver born in Preston. During the Industrial Revolution Preston grew rapidly due to the expansion of textile manufacturing and its development as an engineering centre.

Preston's textile sector fell into decline from the mid-20th century and, in common with other post-industrial towns in the north of England, had to deal with economic deprivation and housing issues. Fortunately new enterprises and light industries coupled with good railway and motorway links have seen a revival for Preston.

Preston has many great buildings and some fine Georgian and Victorian houses. It also has two fine parks, Avenham and Miller Park. Today it is a vibrant shopping centre with all of the main high street stores and a multitude of excellent places to eat.

5. Carlisle

Carlisle (www.carlisle.gov.uk) is the county town of Cumbria, the administrative centre of both Carlisle City Council and Cumbria County Council. It is the largest town in Cumbria with a population of over 100,000 people. Carlisle is located at the confluence of the rivers Eden, Caldew and Petteril, 10 miles (16 km) south of the Scottish border.

The early history of Carlisle is marked by its status as a Roman settlement, established to serve the forts on Hadrian's Wall. During the Middle Ages, because of its closeness to the Scottish border, Carlisle became an important military stronghold. Carlisle Castle was built in 1092 by William Rufus, and once served as a prison for Mary, Queen of Scots. The castle now houses the museums of the Duke of Lancaster's Regiment and the Border Regiment. In the early 12th century Henry I allowed the foundation of a priory in Carlisle which is the present Carlisle Cathedral. The cathedral is well worth visiting and shows many signs of the long border conflict. Carlisle has a turbulent history, being claimed by both the English and the Scots with armies surging backwards and forwards across the disputed border.

During the Industrial Revolution Carlisle became a densely populated mill town. This combined with its strategic position allowed for the development of Carlisle as an important railway town, at one time seven railway companies sharing Carlisle railway station!

Nicknamed the Border City, Carlisle remains the main cultural, commercial and industrial centre for north Cumbria. It is home to the University of Cumbria and a number of museums and heritage centres.

DAY 1: PRESTON TO HURST GREEN
The River Ribble.

DAY 1: PRESTON TO HURST GREEN

This walk follows the route of the Ribble Way and can be turned into a day walk by catching the bus from Hurst Green (last bus 7.10pm) to Whalley and thence to Preston (www.traveline.info). Directions for this walk are from Preston Railway station. For those tempted to take their car be warned that Preston traffic can be very heavy. Refreshments can be obtained at the Riverside Cafe/ Pavilion soon after the start of the walk. The cafe is open, 10am till 5pm where you can get a breakfast, hot meal or sandwiches for a reasonable price and read all about the history of Avenham Park on the excellent wall displays. Leaving here by 10.30am at the latest you should be at the Roman Museum in Ribchester before 4pm if you only take a couple of short breathers. Alternatively you can split the walk into three by stopping at the excellent Brockholes wildlife centre and restaurant after five miles. In Ribchester itself The Potters Barn (closed Mondays from November to March) is personally recommended for refreshments but closes at 5pm (www.potters-barn.com). If you are running late the Ribchester Arms is open for food and refreshments until 9.30pm. (www.theribchesterarms.com). In Hurst Green, as far as I can ascertain, there are only three options for accommodation; The Bayley Arms - good food, friendly service and real ale, Tel 01254 826 478 (www.bayleyarms.co.uk). The Shireburn Arms, Tel 01254 826 678 (www.shireburnarmshotel.com). The Fold B&B, Tel 01254 826 252.

DISTANCE:	17 miles.
ASCENT:	850'
TERRAIN:	Short section of streets, quiet roads and lanes, riverside paths, tracks and good field paths. Can be muddy but not difficult. One short section with undergrowth.
TIME:	6.5 hours (5.5 hours to Ribchester).
START:	Preston Railway Station.
MAPS:	OS Explorer 286 Blackpool & Preston; OS Explorer 287 West Pennine Moors.

FGS Grading
Grading is T5 [D2, N1, T1, R1, H0]

Distance	2	12-18 miles
Navigation	1	Basic navigation skills needed
Terrain	1	50-75% on graded track or path
Remoteness	1	Countryside in fairly close proximity to habitation
Height gain	0	Less than 100 ft per mile

N

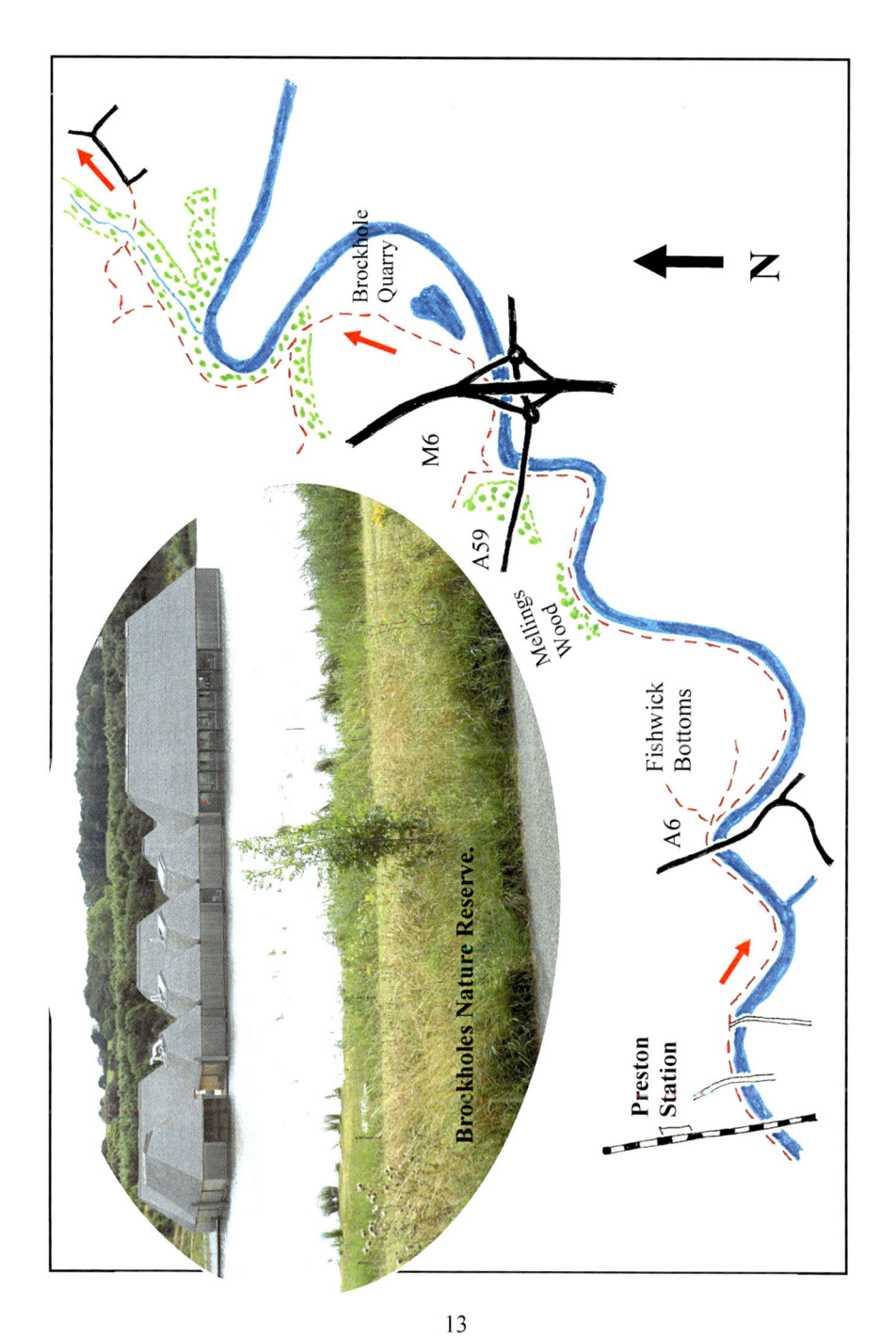

Brockhole Quarry

M6

A59

Mellings Wood

Fishwick Bottoms

A6

Preston Station

Brockholes Nature Reserve.

The River Ribble at Ribchester.

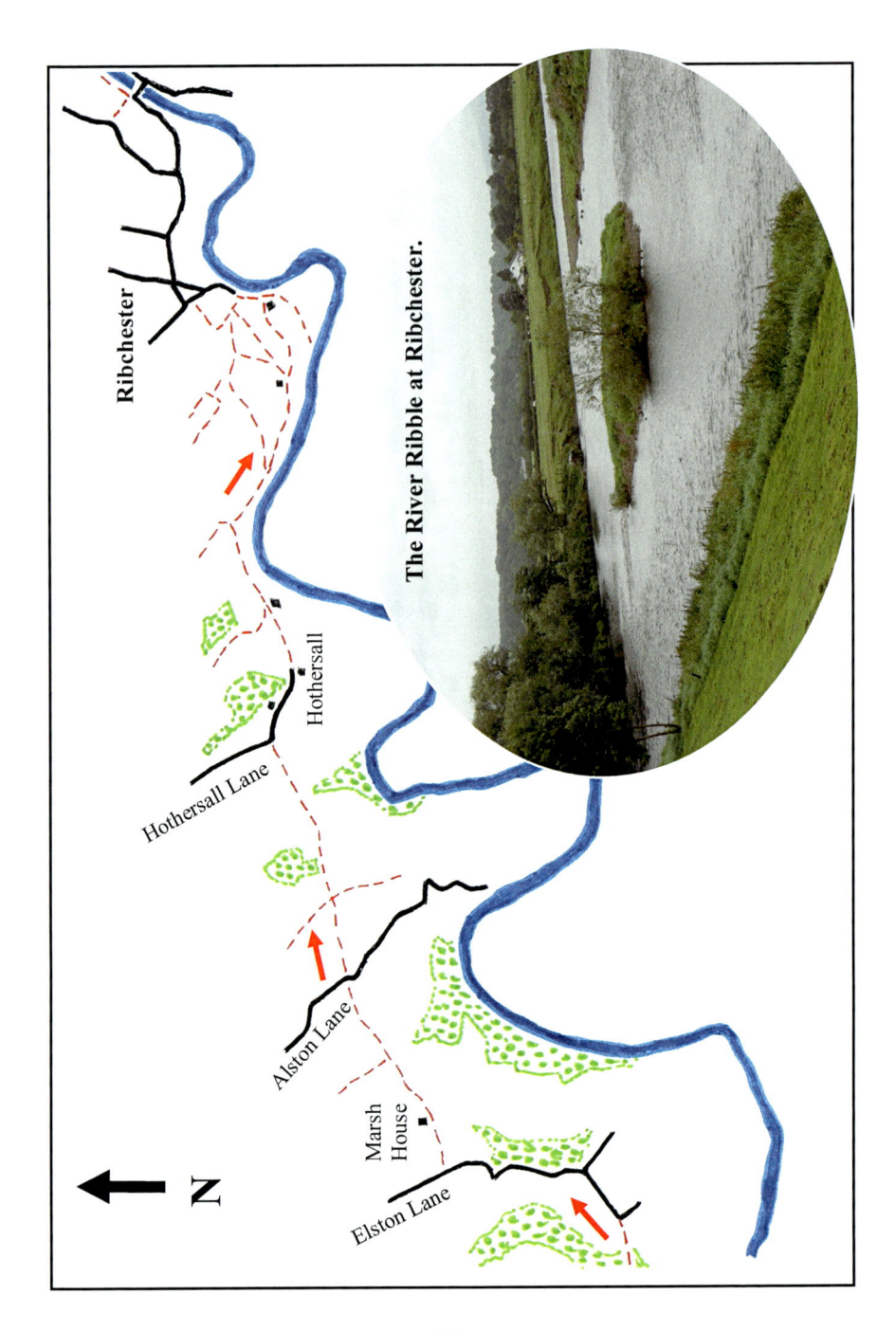

Hurst Green

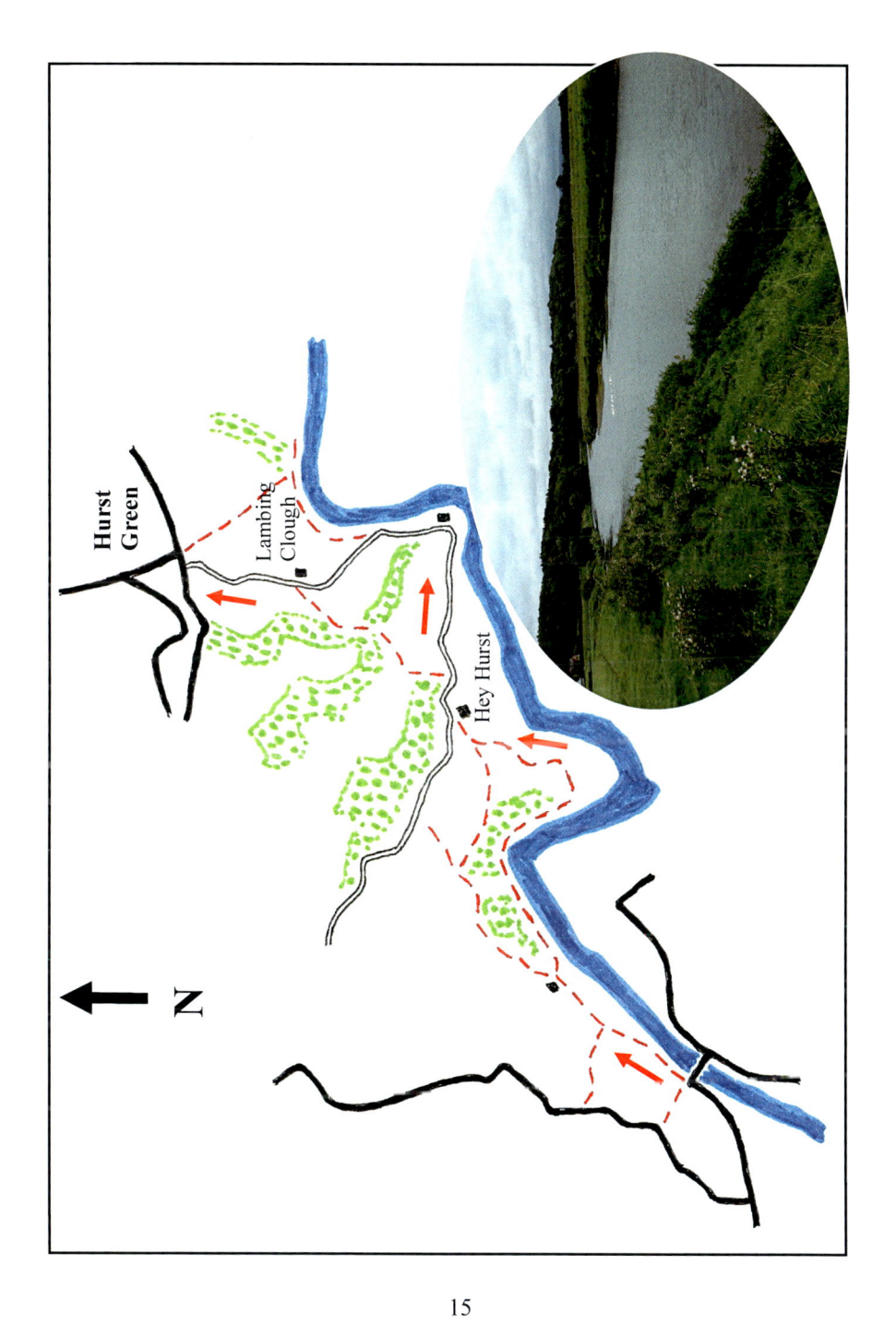

Lambing Clough

Hey Hurst

N

THE WALK

1. Take the main exit out of Preston Railway Station **[SD534 291]** up the ramp and turn right onto Fishergate. Take the 4th right onto Chapel Street to pass Winckley Square.

Winckley Square is the finest example of a privately planned Georgian development with open space in the north of England. Home to the rich and locally famous including Thomas Miller, whose son was responsible for the building of Avenham Park. For a fascinating history of Winckley Square and Preston itself there is a very informative website at www.winckleysquare.org.uk.

2. Carry straight on at the end into Avenham Park. Bear left just before the Boer War Memorial, following the signs for the Riverside Walk and passing the newly restored Japanese Gardens on the right hand side. On the left hand side is the Pavilion/Riverside Cafe.

In the Japanese Gardens you will see a plaque recording the history of the Mormons in Preston. Their first baptisms conducted in Britain were carried out here in the Ribble in 1837.

3. Immediately behind the Pavilion is the Riverside Walk and the start of the section of this walk which follows the Ribble Way. Turn left onto the Riverside Walk and follow the path. Pass a footbridge and continue along the riverside path.

The footbridge is the old tramway bridge which used to connect the two halves of the Lancaster canal (www.alucard.co.uk/lancaster) using horse drawn trucks and stationary steam engines for the steep incline to the bridge. The Lancaster Canal walk is a pleasant walk, especially in the autumn.

4. Cross the A6 **[SD553 288]** and follow the track on the right hand side of the Shawes Arms to a fork. Cross over a stile on your right and follow the riverbank. The path continues along the riverbank, passing the edge of Melling's Wood, where there is a new tarmac path and a picnic table with a beautiful rural view. Continue past a golf course and pass under the A59 **[SD576 300]** and onto a track passing the right hand side of some farm buildings. Turn right onto a track along the riverbank and pass beneath the M6 and the slip road bridges.

The Preston Bypass was Britain's first motorway, opened by Harold Macmillan in 1958.

5. Turn left and follow the Ribble Way signs along a track, bear right and carry straight on, passing through Brockholes Wetlands Centre. Turn right at a large metal gate to visit the centre and restaurant.

This is a major breeding site for over 53 species of bird. The visitor centre on the right hand side, which includes a café [SD588 309], provides excellent food and drink. Should you plan to stop off here you will have to start your day earlier. (www.brockholes.org).

6. Follow the track until you reach some woods. At the perimeter of the woods bear right and turn left to climb through Boilton Wood. On emerging from the trees **[SD584 315]** bear right and follow the fringe of the wood along a clearly defined path. The path continues for some distance, dipping in and out of the woods until you cross a stile.

7. Bear right across the field, following the bridleway signs. Cross a succession of stiles. Eventually a well defined path takes you into Tun Brook Wood.

Remnant of ancient woodlands, which date from the end of the last ice age. Native trees include alder, ash, hazel, holly and oak. This is also the site of an undiscovered crossing of the Roman road from Ribchester to Dowbridge near Kirkham.

8. A path drops steeply down to a footbridge **[SD591 325]** then climbs out to emerge into fields. Head for a gate in the top left corner to join Elston Lane. Turn left onto the lane and left at the next junction. Continue for approximately ¾ of a mile and near to the top of the rise turn right onto a farm track clearly marked Ribble Way **[SD598 336]**. Pass Marsh House farm and straight on through a gate along a hedged green track. Bear left and then go over a stone stile next to a gate on the right hand side. Continue straight ahead alongside the fence to the next field. Cross a footbridge and straight ahead, passing a pond and heading for the left hand side of a house on the far side. Cross a stile onto Alston Lane.

Tun Brook.

9. Cross Alston Lane to a stile opposite and follow the electricity poles to the 3rd pole. Turn left and cross a footbridge over a brook **[SD612 342]**. Carry straight on to cross another brook **[SD613 343]**. Carry straight on to a gap in an electric fence, a stile and footbridge. Continue straight on to a tree and follow the fence on the right hand side to drop down into a wooded gulley to cross a footbridge. Keep to the left hand field boundary crossing 4 stiles to eventually join a track beside a cottage. Follow the track to Hothersall Lane **[SD623 347]**.

10. Turn right onto Hothersall Lane, dropping down and curving left past Hothersall Lodge Field Studies Centre. The lane ends and you continue past Hothersall Hall, through two gates onto a fenced track. As the track bears left cross a ladder stile on the right and head up a wooded bank. Skirt left past and then through the trees **[SD636 350]**. Head for a gate near to the bottom right hand corner of the field. Continue through the fields to join a hedged track, past a farm and then St Wilfrid's Church into Ribchester.

St Wilfrid's Church.

Saint Wilfrid's Church (www.saintwilfrids.org.uk) is built on the site of a Roman fort, the oldest part dating from 1193 with many subsequent interesting additions.

11. Bear left into the village past the Roman Museum and then the White Bull and then left again to the Potters Barn. 13 miles.

Ribchester Roman Museum (open until 5pm), built on the site of the Roman Headquarters, is small but extremely informative, well worth a visit (www.ribchesterromanmuseum.org). The 4 pillars which form the White Bull's porch are from a Roman temple (www.white-bull.co.uk).

12. Turn back from the Potters Barn and turn left past a post office and village shop and turn right at the Black Bull. Pass the Ribchester Arms and cross the stone bridge over the brook **[SD654 354]**. Carry on along the road as far as Ribchester Bridge. Do not cross the bridge but continue straight ahead along the track into a farmyard. Turn right before a converted barn and cross a ladder stile **[SD667 364]** to continue along a path beside the river. Pass below Stewart's Wood and through Haugh Wood.

13. At the end of the wood bear left to a stile and then left up a steep grass bank **[SD676 362]**. Walk over the hill and aim for the left hand edge of Pendle Hill in the distance. Drop down to a gate at the bottom of the dip and then bear left to head for the far top left corner of the next field **[SD677 366]**. Bear right to reach a track, turn right and then immediate left and pass through a gate on the opposite side. Follow the left hand boundary down to a footbridge at the bottom of Clough Bank Wood **[SD680 367]**.

14. Follow the right hand field boundary over 2 stiles and straight onto a gate into a green track which bears left through Trough House farmyard **[SD687 368]** and on to Lambing Clough, ignoring the sign for the Ribble Way path on the right. The track becomes a lane which leads into Hurst Green. Turn right and the Shireburn Arms **[SD685 379]** is immediately on your right. Turn left up the hill to reach the Bayley Arms. Continue a short distance and turn right into Smithy Row for The Fold B&B.

Stoneyhurst is probably most famous for the Jesuit College. J R R Tolkien regularly stayed in the grounds and also frequented the Shireburn Arms. This area is reputed to be the setting for The Lord of the Rings.

DAY 2: HURST GREEN TO GISBURN
Cromwell's Bridge from Lower Hodder Bridge.

DAY 2: HURST GREEN TO GISBURN

This walk continues to follow the Ribble Way but, as with most long distance walks, you cannot rely on the waymarkers. Once again this can be turned into a day walk by getting the bus to Whalley and then Hurst Green as per yesterday's walk and then return to Preston via the regular bus service, details of which are at http://getdown.org.uk/bus/bus/280.htm. Hill Crest Tea Rooms, approximately 2 hours into the walk, are personally recommended for hot food and drinks but closed Thursday and Friday, Tel 01254 826 573. Further into the walk at Edisford Bridge, you can turn left over the bridge and walk 300 yards to the Edisford Bridge Hotel. Tel 01200 422 637. Some $5^1/_2$ hours into the walk the Spread Eagle at Sawley is open for food 12-2pm (if you've made a very early start!) and drinks all day, Tel 01200 441 202 (www.spreadeaglesawley.co.uk). The White Bull in Gisburn provides excellent value accommodation, Tel 01200 445 155 (www.whitebullgisburn.co.uk). The only other accommodation I could find is Park House B&B, Tel 01200 445 269 (www.parkhousegisburn.co.uk).

DISTANCE: 19 miles.
ASCENT: 535'
TERRAIN: Riverside and field paths/tracks. Some road and lane walking.
TIME: 9 hours
START: Hurst Green
MAPS: OS Explorer 287 West Pennine Moors, OL41 Forest of Bowland and Ribblesdale

FGS Grading
Grading is T5 [D2, N1, T1, R1, H0]

Distance	2	12-18 miles
Navigation	1	Basic navigation skills needed
Terrain	1	50-75% on graded track or path
Remoteness	1	Countryside in fairly close proximity to habitation
Height gain	0	Less than 100 ft per mile

The River Hodder joins the River Ribble.

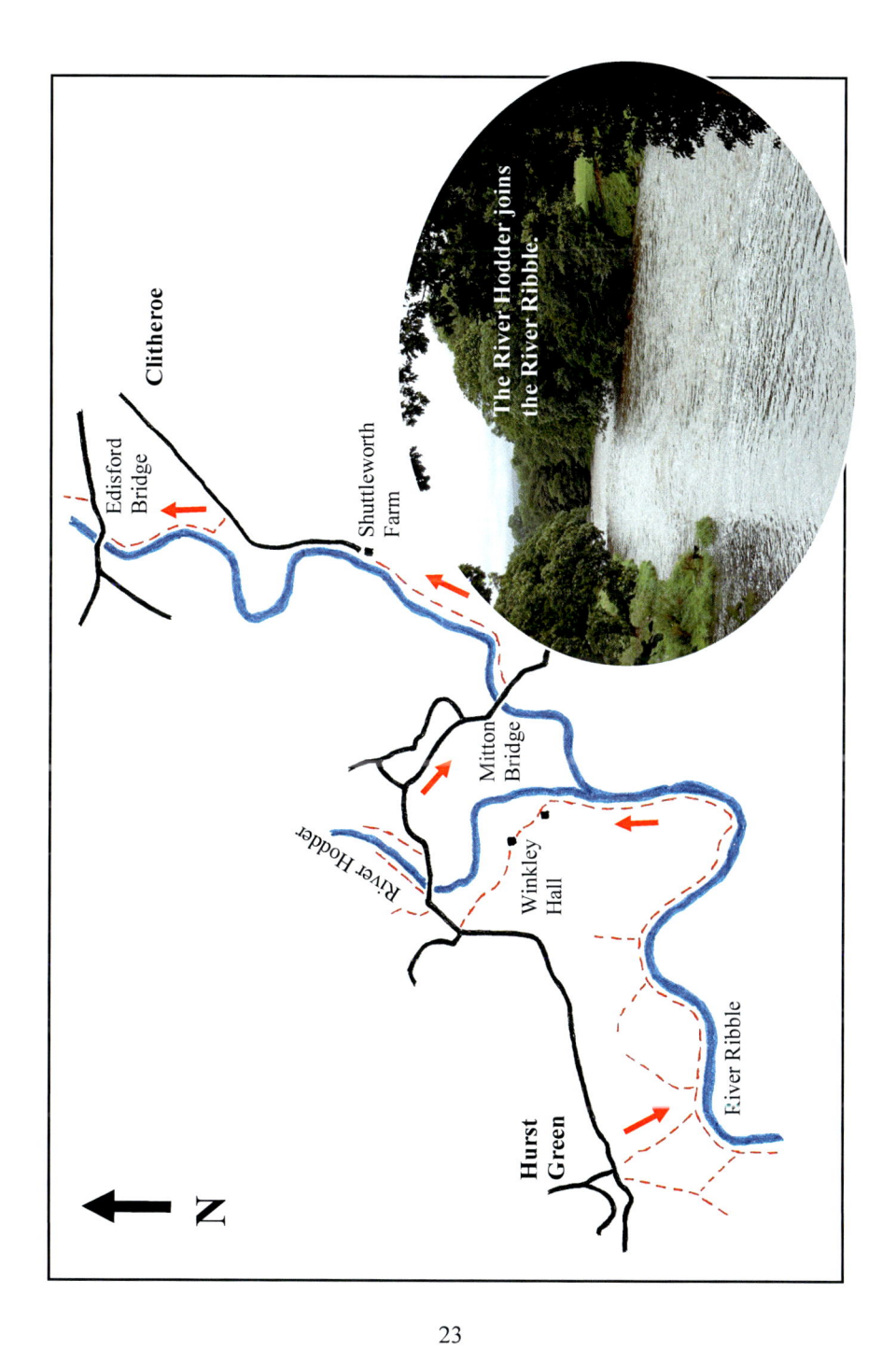

N

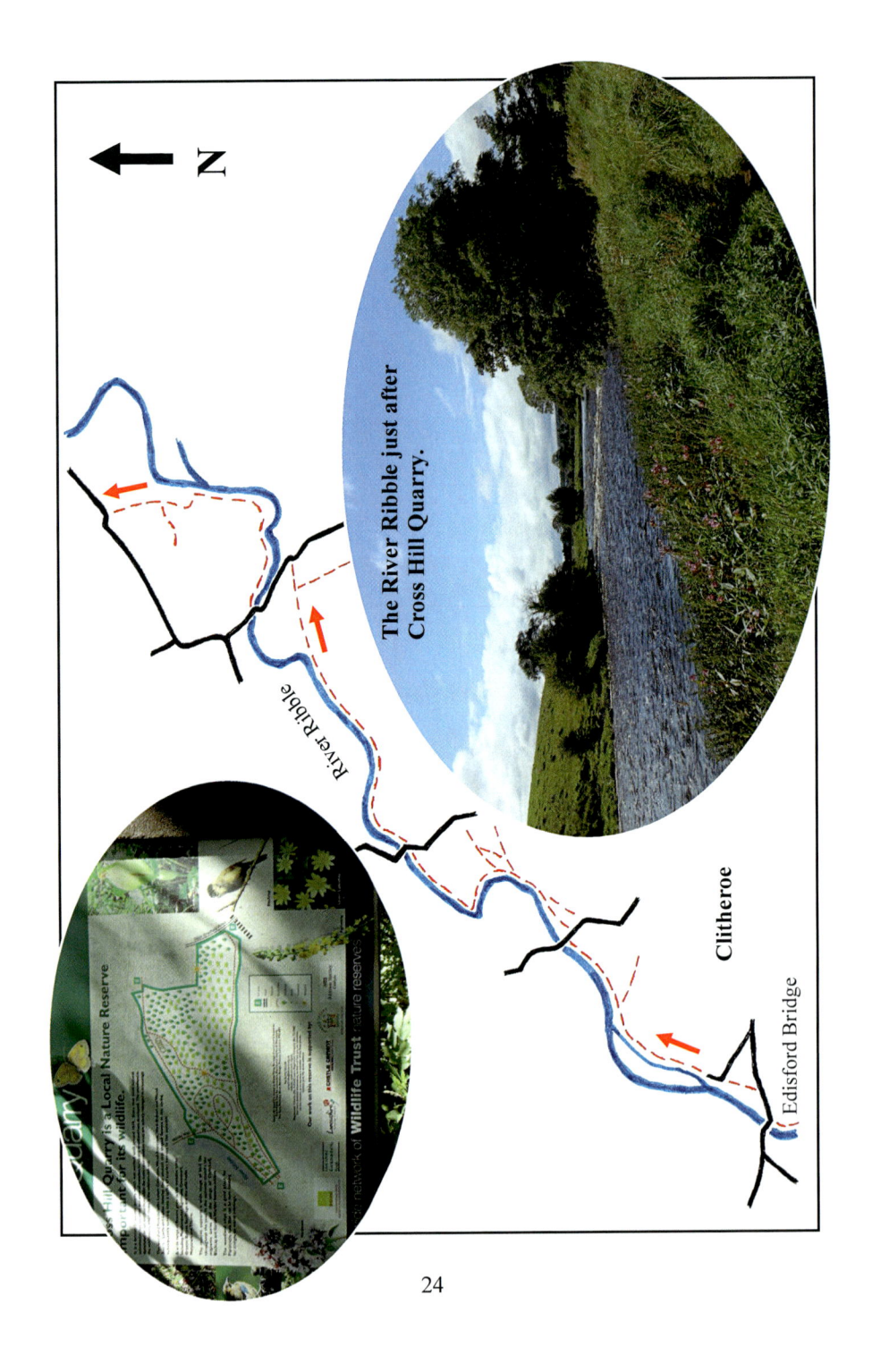

The River Ribble just after Cross Hill Quarry.

River Ribble

Clitheroe

Edisford Bridge

24

St Mary the Virgin, Gisburn.

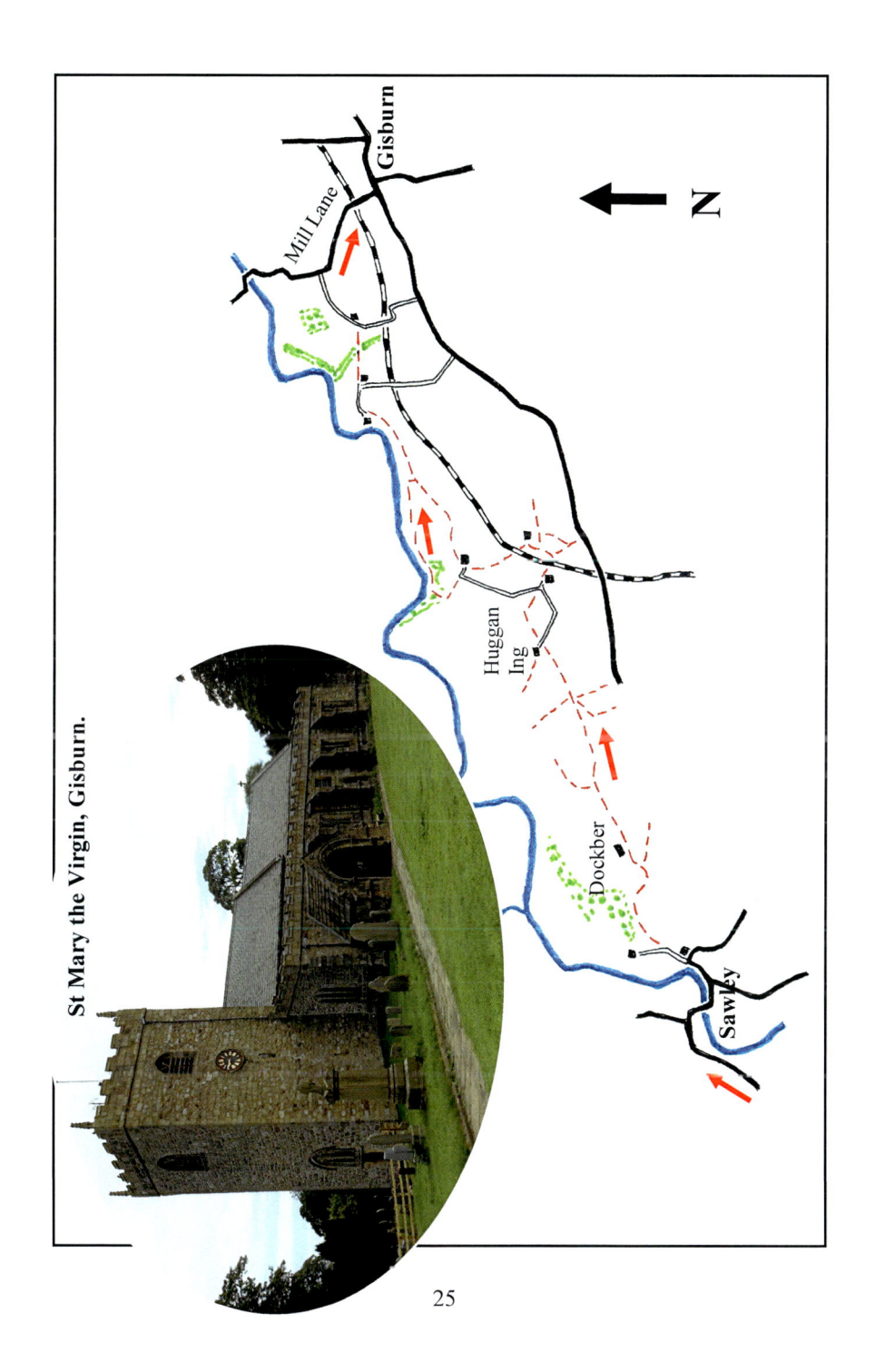

THE WALK

1. Take the path marked through the car park at the left hand side side of the Shireburn Arms **[SD685 379]**. Go through a wooden gate and follow the right hand field boundary, halfway down the field the path switches to the other side of the field boundary. Veer right at the end of the field to cross a stile and a footbridge. Turn left onto the Ribble Way path which leads to a footbridge over Dean Brook. Continue along the riverside path and eventually join a tarmac lane which continues to follow the river. The lane bears right and then left and a sign diverts you right onto a grass path on the riverbank. The path becomes a track reaching to Winckley Hall Farm. The track goes left and right through the farmyard and then climbs through the trees. Continue past the entrance to Winckley Hall but as the track bears left pass through a kissing gate on the right **[SD706 386]**.

2. Head across the field to another stile then straight ahead to join and then follow the edge of the wood. Cross a stile, pass through a gateway on the right hand side and then diagonally left to a lane **[SD701 390]**. Turn right onto the lane (signposted Whalley) and follow it to cross Lower Hodder bridge.

The bridge to the right is an old packhorse bridge called Cromwell's Bridge, because his army crossed this bridge on their way to fight the Battle of Preston at Gisburn.

3. At the next junction **[SD710 394]** bear right (signposted Whalley) to reach Hill Crest Tea Rooms on the left hand side. All Hallows Church lies immediately behind the tea rooms.

All Hallows Church, which dates from 1270, is regarded by some experts as one of England's finest examples of a medieval church.
www.thethreefishes.com/hallows-church.htm

4. Cross Mitton Bridge to the Aspinall Arms and turn left at the side of the pub outbuildings onto the Ribble Way path **[SD717 387]**. The path continues through a kissing gate and then over a footbridge. Bear left to a River Board building and then follow the track. Pass an aqueduct and join a field track to Shuttleworth Farm. Pass through a kissing gate and across a small paddock to join a farm access road which becomes a lane. The lane bears right (a shaded path runs parallel to the lane on the left hand side) and crosses a stream where

All Hallow's Church, Great Mitton.

you turn left for Siddows Farm **[SD728 406]**. Take the right fork where the track splits and then immediately turn left through a small wooden gate. Follow the fenced path to drop down to rejoin the riverbank. Continue to Edisford Bridge.

5. Just before the bridge turn right onto the footpath and continue along before crossing via the pelican crossing to the leisure centre. Take the main drive **[SD729 415]** between the swimming pool and the tennis hall and bear right across the playing fields towards a lamppost. Pass a retirement home on the right hand side into Low Moor village. Turn left onto the main street which immediately bears right at a junction and then take the upper branch at the next fork. Continue past the Wesleyan Sunday School on the left hand side and past the houses where the road becomes a track between allotments and smallholdings **[SD730 420]**.

6. Continue along the track and upstream passing Waddow Hall on the opposite bank. At Brungerley Bridge turn right and after 100 yards turn left into Brungerley Park **[SD739 427]**. Keep to the upper route and then bear left to enter into Crosshill Quarry Nature Reserve. Bear left to keep to the riverside path **[SD743 432]**.

Waddow Hall, is a 17th century manor house used since 1927 by the Girl

Guides (now the Guide Association). Abandoned as a working quarry in the early 1900s, Cross Hill is a good example of natural change on a man-made site and has since become an exceptional refuge for wildlife. www.lancswt.org.uk (downloadable leaflets available).

7. Continue to Bradford Bridge and cross the road, passing through a kissing gate opposite. Continue over several stiles and after less than a mile move away from the river by crossing a stile to the top of a bank and the path continues between the trees. The path leaves the wood and keeps to the edge of the field. Follow this round to a wooden gate which takes you to a lane **[SD765 446]**. Cross the lane and follow the clearly marked path to Grindleton Bridge. Once over the bridge turn right onto the riverside path.

8. Continue to a stile just after where Swanside Beck joins the river on the other side. The path bears left away from the river to a second stile. Bear right across the field to a ladder stile at the far end. Climb up to another stile, then cross the next field to a stone stile to the left of a gate in the top wall **[SD768 460]**. Turn right onto the lane into Sawley. Cross the bridge into Sawley and bear left as you pass the Spread Eagle onto the minor lane beside the river.

9. Pass through a gateway along the drive to Sawley Lodge. As the drive bears left turn right through a narrow gate **[SD779 468]**. Climb up and turn left onto the track which passes through West Dockber Farm. Continue climbing almost to the top. Pass through a gate on the right **[SD790 473]** and bear left to the bottom corner of a plantation. Pass through a metal gate by the ruins of a stone building. Turn left along the edge of the trees to another stile next to some metal gates. Head diagonally right (past a sword embedded in a boulder!) to join a track and carry on with the fence on your right **[SD795 475]**.

10. Continue along a line of hawthorn bushes to reach a track to Huggan Ing farm. Cross to a small metal gate and continue along the old field boundary. Pass through another small metal gate and head diagonally right to Gisburn Cotes Hall farm **[SD801 477]**. Pass through a gate in the corner of the field and turn left past the front of the farmhouse and over a railway bridge.

This is the restored Settle to Carlisle railway (www.settle-carlisle.co.uk). Regular services are diesel but there are occasional steam specials (www.uksteam.info).

11. Immediately over the bridge fork left to Gisburn Cotes Farm. Once in the yard, and before the building, pass through a gate on the left and over the grassed railway bridge ahead **[SD804 478]**. Over the bridge turn diagonally right towards another farm and cross stiles to the left of the farmhouse **[SD803 481]**. Turn left onto a track. Follow the track to a bend where you carry straight on over a stile **[SD801 483]**. Follow the fence down to the top of a wooded gulley where you cross another two, almost hidden stiles onto a steep stepped path down to the Ribble. Take great care as this is very slippery.

12. Turn alongside the river and after a short distance cross a stile and follow a rising track. Follow the clearly marked Ribble Way signs to eventually join a tarmac track **[SD813 488]**. Just before the buildings bear left over a stile next to a gate, then head to the crest of the field. Drop down to a gate in the left fence **[SD816 489]**. Follow the path to cross a sleeper bridge over a stream **[SD817 489]** and climb through the trees to a field where you bear right to a small gate just to the right of Coppice Farm (almost totally hidden by trees). Pass through Coppice Farm and take a tarmac track over a cattle grid which joins the drive from Copy House and out to Mill Lane **[SD822 491]**. Turn right onto the lane and follow it for ½ a mile up to Gisburn **[SD829 488]**.

Gisburn has its own excellent website at www.gisburn.org.uk

The White Bull, Gisburn.

DAY 3: GISBURN TO MALHAM
Attermire Scar.

DAY 3: GISBURN TO MALHAM

The start of this walk continues to follow the Ribble Way but then diverts eastwards towards limestone country. It passes through the village of Long Preston (www.longpreston.info) after 8.5 miles where refreshments can be obtained. The village post office appears to offer excellent value food and drink from 10am to 4pm but has been closed all three times that I have passed through. The Maypole Inn (www.maypole.co.uk) has excellent, but more expensive, refreshments if the tearooms are closed. The walk continues through Langcliffe and Attermire Scars nature reserve and onto the Pennine Bridleway into Malham. From Malham we pick up the Pennine Way at arguably one of its most beautiful points and follow it for another 7 days. Provided that you make a reasonably early start, and do not dally too long at the Maypole Inn, this can be turned into a day walk by catching the bus from Malham to Skipton @ 16.45 (Skipton 17.20) and then Skipton (Stand 3) @ 17.30 (Gisburn 17.58). It would however be a shame not to stop in Malham as it is a delightful village with an excellent website (www.malhamdale.com). This is a very popular place to stay so book accommodation well in advance. Fortunately there is a wide selection of accommodation, all listed on the website.

DISTANCE: 18.5 miles.
ASCENT: 680'
TERRAIN: Field paths and tracks. Some quiet road walking.
TIME: 7 hours
START: Gisburn
MAP: OL41 Forest of Bowland and Ribblesdale

FGS Grading
Grading is T5[D2, N1, T1, R1, H0]

Distance	2	12-18 miles
Navigation	1	Basic navigation skills needed
Terrain	1	50-75% on graded track or path
Remoteness	1	Countryside in fairly close proximity to habitation
Height gain	0	Less than 100 ft per mile

N

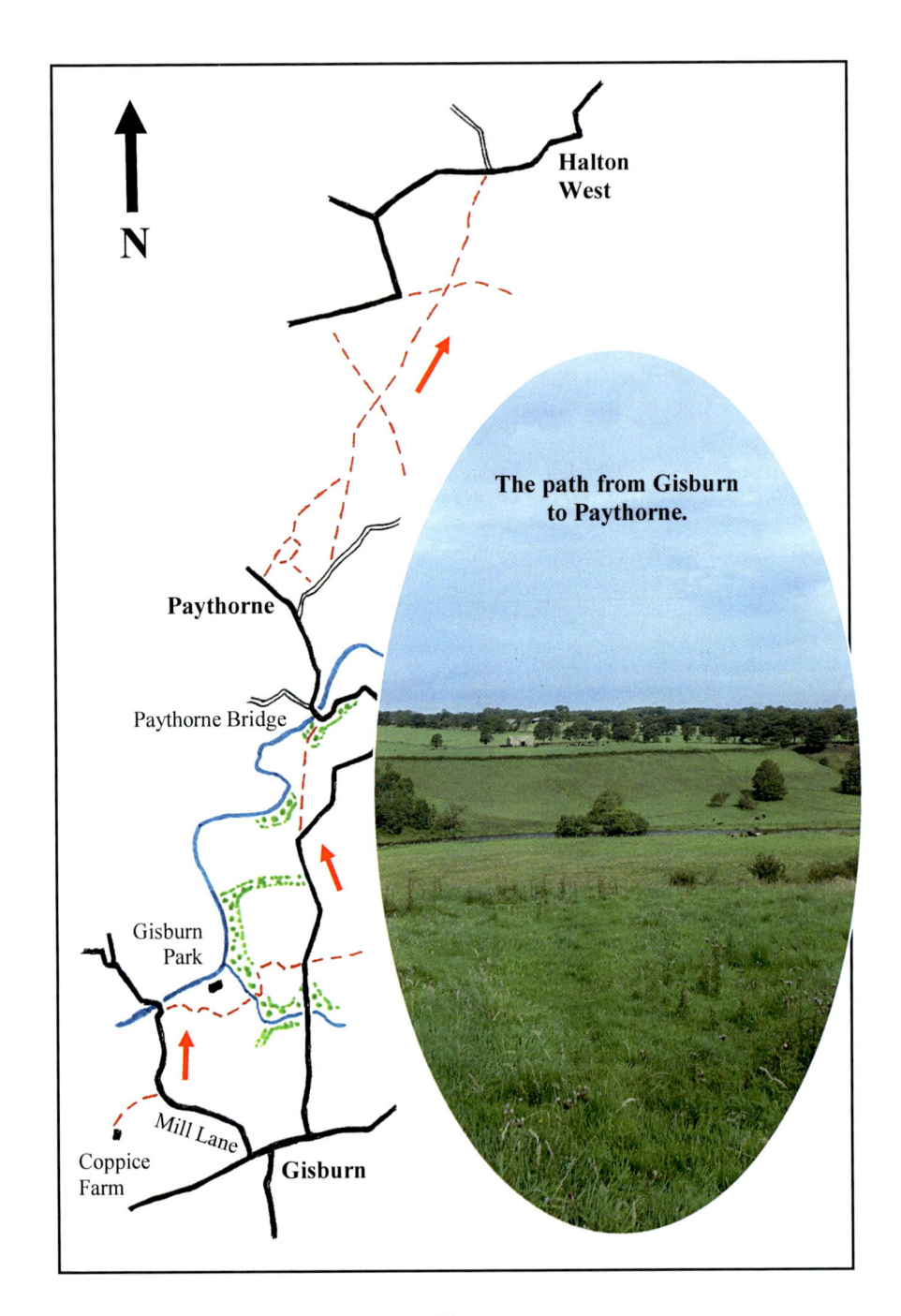

Halton West

The path from Gisburn to Paythorne.

Paythorne

Paythorne Bridge

Gisburn Park

Mill Lane

Coppice Farm

Gisburn

Long Preston Beck.

34

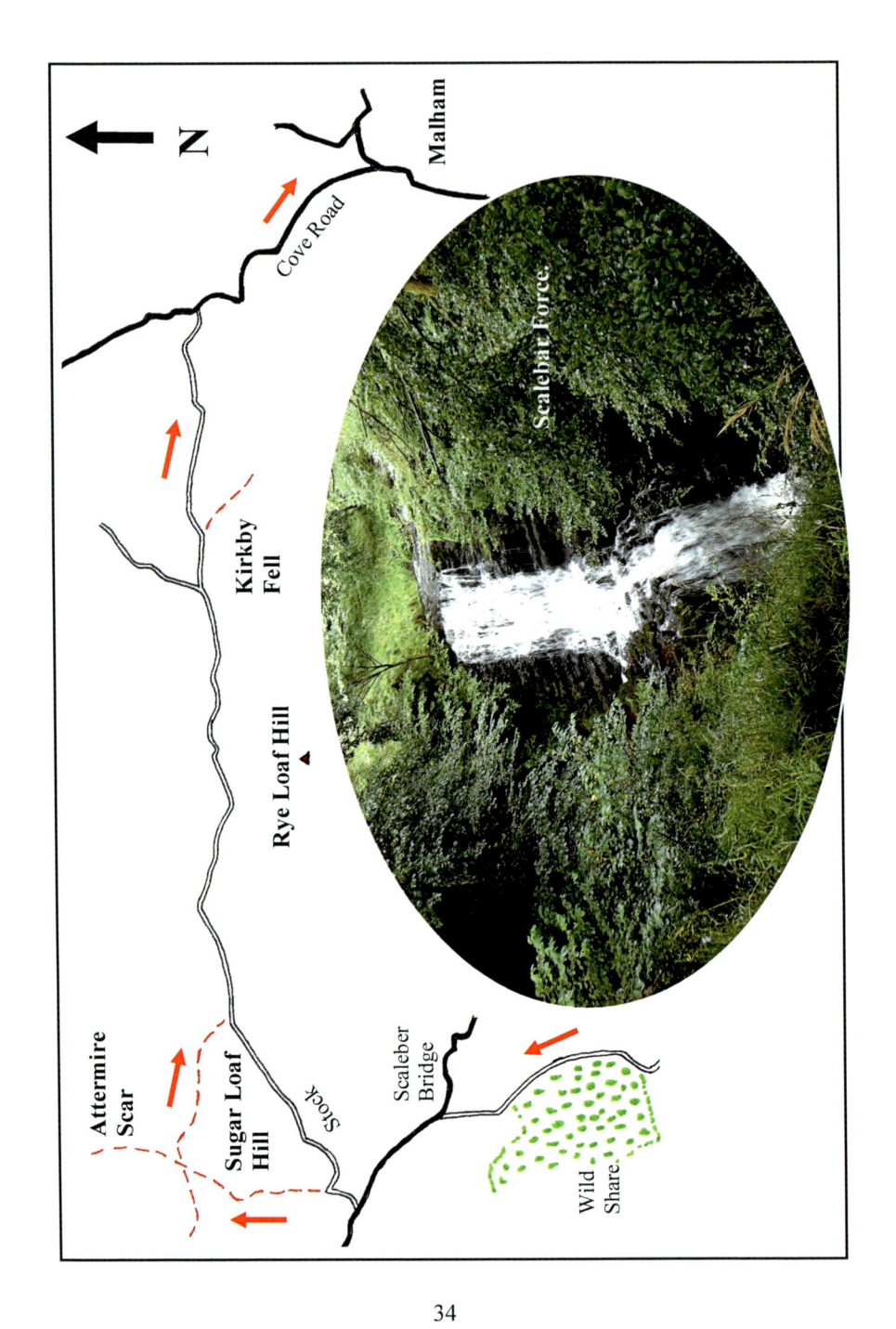

THE WALK

1. From the White Bull turn right and return down Mill Lane. At the very bottom turn right (signposted Pennine Bridleway) **[SD828 488]** and walk through Gisburn Park. Follow this track which leaves the woods at the top and continue to the A682 **[SD830 498]**.

Gisburne Park was built by the Lister family in the 18th century. Wild white cattle grazed here and this is where the White Bull gets its name from. For more history of Gisburne Park and Gisburn village visit www.gisburn.org.uk

2. Follow a path at the edge of the field alongside the road. Continue over the hill to a gate and bear right to cross a stream. Carry on alongside the field boundary to another gate in the far-right corner. Bear left, aiming for the right-hand edge of a tree crowned mound **[SD830 508]**. Pass through gates which lead onto a path at the edge of a ditch.

The impressive earthworks are all that remains of the early Norman Castle Haugh, known locally as Cromwell's Basin, again for more details visit www.gisburn.org.uk

3. Follow the bridleway alongside the right-hand fence to the corner of a wood. Follow a path through the trees to a lane at the bottom. Cross Paythorne Bridge and follow the lane uphill to Paythorne village.

Salmon Sunday is the nearest one to November 20th, when folk gather at the Paythorne Bridge to see the arrival of the salmon.

4. Just before the Buck Inn, at a telephone box, turn right up a bridleway **[SD830 518]**. Pass Manor House Farm, turn left up a track clearly marked Pennine Bridleway / Ribble Way. Continue along the track through two gates and bear right and follow the track over two stiles to a brook where the track bears right. Do not bear right but pass through a gate and over the brook, turning left before a stile (signposted Pennine Bridleway).

5. Continue on a clearly defined path, crossing a footbridge **[SD835 530]** where you should ignore the Ribble Way signs but continue to follow the Pennine Bridleway signs to Halton West.

The River Ribble from Paythorne Bridge.

6. Turn left just before Town End Farm onto a track **[SD841 543]**. Continue on this track to Low Scales Farm. Just before reaching it go right through a gate, bear left to a stile, bear left to a small wooden gate. Bear left to another gate, over a ditch through another gate then head up the field. Continue through another field to pass through a kissing gate and follow the field boundary. Cross a stile to the right of the second large metal gate and continue diagonally left to join a track alongside a wooded clough **[SD827 556]**.

7. Continue along the track which becomes Todmanhaw Lane and winds across the fields until it reaches a lane at Cow Bridge **[SD827 569]**. Turn right to cross the bridge and continue past the railway station into Long Preston. Turn left onto the busy main road and cross to the other side via the pelican crossing.

8. Turn right just before the Maypole Inn **[SD834 582]** and continue up the road until it bears right. Turn left up the lane signposted "Private - no through road" and follow it all the way down to Long Preston Beck. Cross the beck via the footbridge **[SD842 586]** and turn left onto the path. The path now runs alongside the beck passing through an open gateway, a gap in a broken wall and over a stile, through a gate and over another stile. Cross the beck via another footbridge, do not cross the second footbridge but turn right and then pass through a small metal gate almost hidden on the left hand side of the gate facing you. Head up the track, pass through a wooden gate in the wall on the right hand side **[SD842 595]** before the next open gateway and carry straight on. Pass through another wooden gate and follow the path to pass between two trees ahead. Follow the path through a gap in the wall, over a small beck and across to run alongside the main beck. Pass through two metal gates and continue along the left hand bank to some obvious stepping stones. Now on the right hand bank pass through another metal gate before the path leads up the bank.

9. Turn left onto the tarmac track and follow it, passing the newly planted Hawes native broadleaf woodland, then Wild Share plantation until you reach the road. Carry straight on passing over Scalebar Bridge **[SD841 625]** and past Scalebar Force. At a junction turn right onto Stockdale Lane (Pennine Bridleway) **[SD836 630]**. Bear left and where the lane bears right continue straight ahead over a stile. Pass between two hills and then veer left around

Attermire Scar.

Sugar Loaf Hill and then bear right with the field boundary and straight on to pass through a gate and turn right onto the path from Settle **[SD839 641]**.

10. Follow this path through Langcliffe and Attermire Scars nature reserve until you turn left onto Stockdale Lane. Follow this to join the Pennine Bridleway. Pass through a large gate, a small gate and then another large gate. Continue to another wooden gate where the Pennine Bridleway turns left but carry on through the gate on the Bridleway for Cove Road. Follow this bridleway all the way to the end **[SD891 640]** and turn right onto Cove Road which leads you into Malham village **[SD901 628]**.

Bridge over Malham Beck.

DAY 4: MALHAM TO HORTON-IN-RIBBLESDALE

The view from Pen-y-Ghent with Whernside in the far distance and the footpath down to Horton.

DAY 4: MALHAM TO HORTON-IN-RIBBLESDALE

The walk now picks up the Pennine Way – but don't assume it will be well waymarked all the way! This is an excellent day's walking through limestone country but does involve some serious climbs for the first time. The route passes Malham Tarn and climbs over Pen-y-Ghent (if the weather is very bad, or exhaustion has set in, it is possible to bypass Pen-y-Ghent). The walk ends in Horton-in-Ribblesdale where you will find the Crown Inn, one of my most favourite inns. There are no refreshments available on today's walk so you will need to carry your own. Accommodation in Horton is surprisingly limited in view of the popularity of this area. If you want to book in at the Crown Hotel, Tel 01729 860209 (www.crown-hotel.co.uk), you may need to book several months in advance. The food is excellent and, if you are a real ale fan, the Theakstons Old Peculier is an outstanding real ale. The Golden Lion, Tel 01729 860206 (www.goldenlionhotel.co.uk) has a selection of rooms and a bunk house with 15 bunks. Another nice bunkhouse is the 3 Peaks Bunkroom (www.3peaksbunkroom.co.uk) 01729 860380. The only other accommodation I have been able to locate, after considerable research on the internet and numerous visits to the village, is the Willows Bed and Breakfast, Tel 01729 860200 (www.thewillowshorton.co.uk).

There is no scheduled bus service from Horton but there are regular trains to Leeds and Carlisle and the local taxi service is Settle Taxis, Tel 01729 822219.

DISTANCE:	15.5 miles.
ASCENT:	3,700'
TERRAIN:	Paths and tracks. A small amount of road and lane walking.
TIME:	8 hours
START:	Malham
MAPS:	OL2 Yorkshire Dales Southern & Western

FGS Grading
Grading is F8 [D2, N1, T1, R2, H2]

Distance	2	12-18 miles
Navigation	1	Basic navigation skills needed
Terrain	1	50-75% on graded track or path
Remoteness	2	Countryside in fairly close proximity to habitation
Height gain	2	Over 125 ft per mile

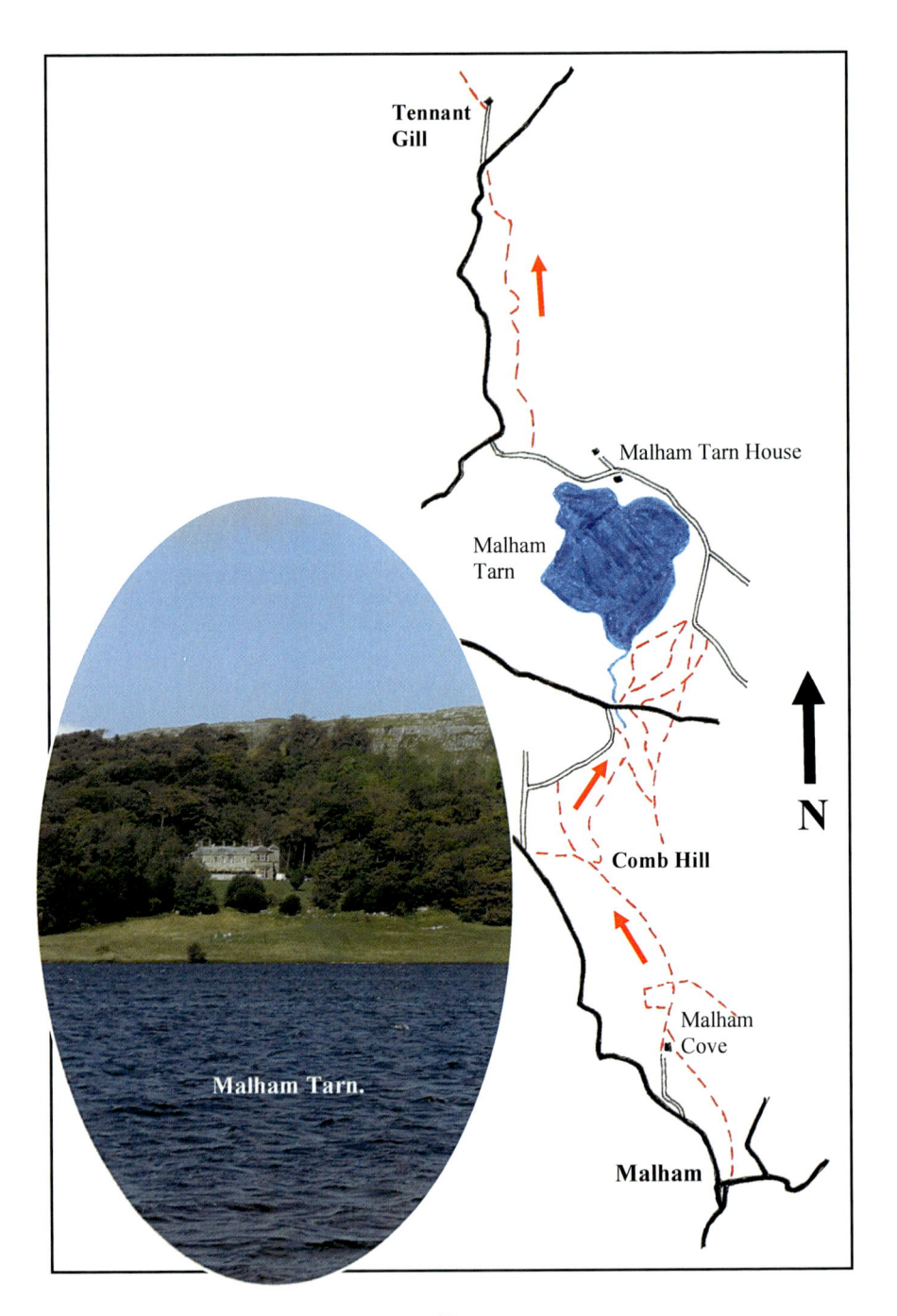

Malham Tarn.
Tennant Gill
Malham Tarn House
Malham Tarn
Comb Hill
Malham Cove
Malham
N

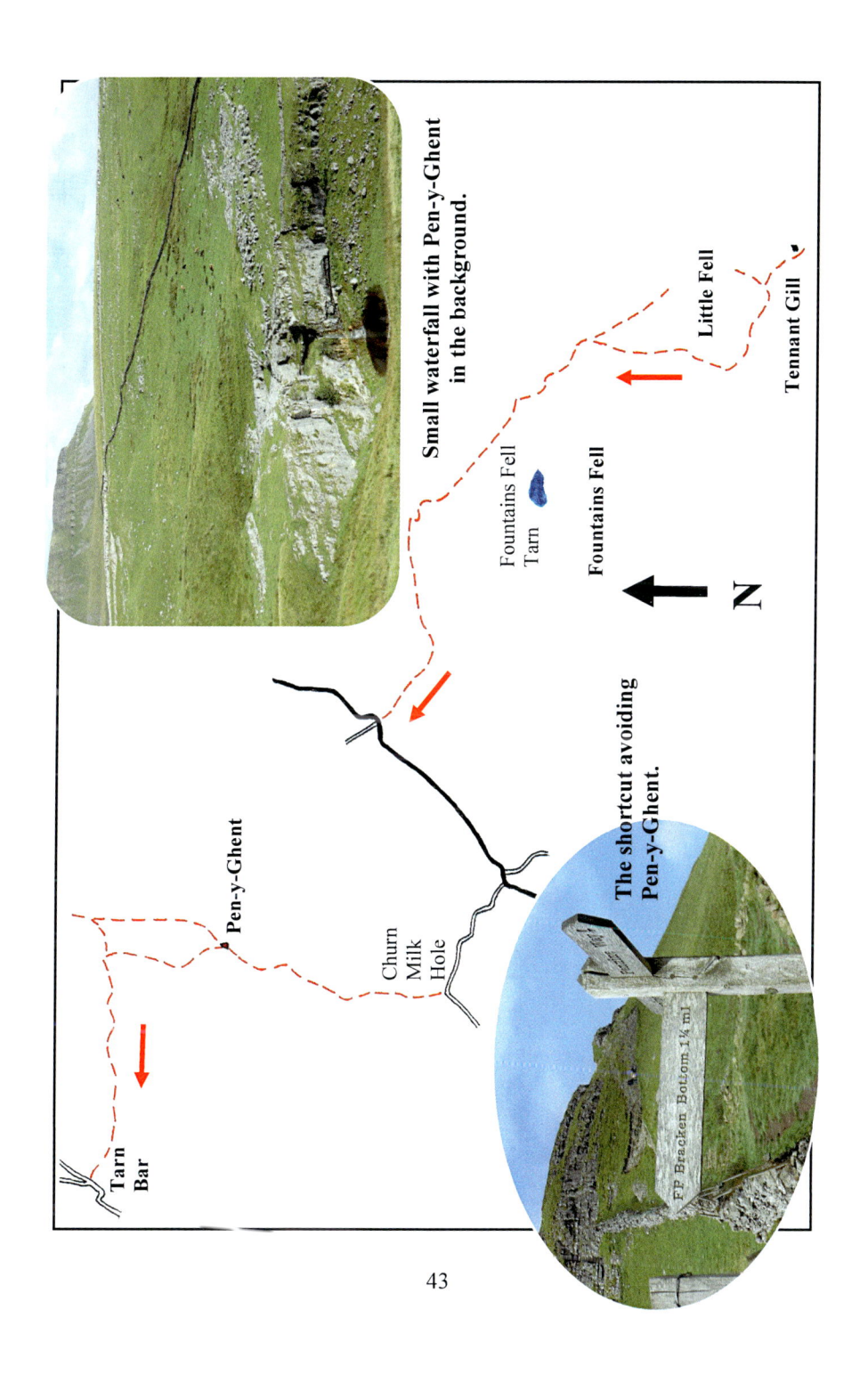

Small waterfall with Pen-y-Ghent in the background.

Little Fell

Tennant Gill

Fountains Fell Tarn

Fountains Fell

N

Pen-y-Ghent

Churn Milk Hole

The shortcut avoiding Pen-y-Ghent.

FP Bracken Bottom 1¼ ml

Tarn Bar

43

The Crown, Horton-in-Ribblesdale.

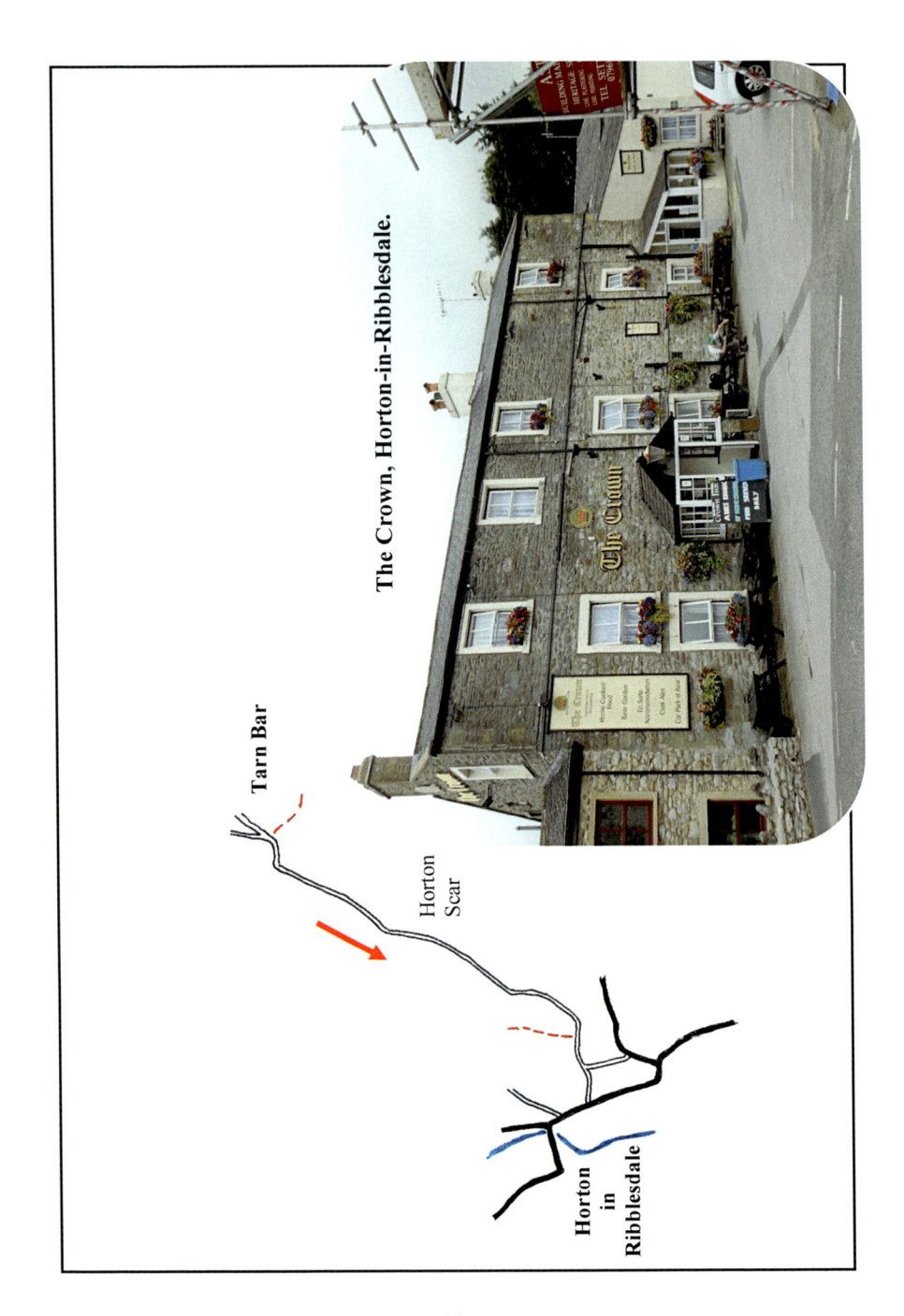

Tarn Bar

Horton Scar

Horton in Ribblesdale

THE WALK

1. Head north along Cove Road and pick up the Pennine Way which forks off to the right onto a pathway which approaches the Cove beside Malham Beck. It then bears left up a stepped path to the clifftop. Pass through a gate, turn left for a few yards and then right across the limestone paving.

The cliff is 230' high and 650' across and was once a waterfall at the end of the last ice age greater in size than the Niagara Falls. The limestone paving is caused by the action of slightly acidic rain over many thousands of years on small grooves and hollows in the limestone, which become 'clints' (the blocks of limestone) and 'grykes' (the gaps) creating a unique habitat for rare wild flowers and ferns.

Malham Cove and, inset, the limestone walls.

2. Continue in the same direction keeping fairly close to the edge until you reach a wall where you turn left **[SD897 642]**, following a sign for the Pennine Way. Cross a stile into Malham Tarn Nature Reserve. Cross another stile, up some stone steps and over another stile, then turn sharp right back on yourself **[SD891 649]**, signposted Pennine Way, to skirt past Comb Hill. Eventually you emerge onto flat grasslands. At the top of a rise, bear right (signposted Malham Tarn) **[SD892 651]** and on reaching a road turn right and then turn left **[SD894 658]** to follow the path to Malham Tarn. At a fork in the indistinct pathway continue straight ahead towards Malham Tarn House in the distance and eventually to the Tarn itself.

Malham Tarn is a natural upland lake which lies on 400 million year old impervious silurian slate. It has a surface area of 150 acres and an average depth of 2.4 metres with a maximum depth of 4.4 metres. The tarn has a reputation for excellent trout and is also home to many water birds including curlews, mallards and greater crested grebe which are protected in a sanctuary on the western shore.

Malham Tarn from the bird hide.

3. The path follows the east shore, cutting diagonally across to a gate where you enter Malham Tarn National Nature Reserve. Follow the track past Malham Tarn House bearing right, left and right into the woods. There is an observation platform on the left hand side which overlooks the Tarn. Shortly after this there is a bird hide - a useful place to change socks on a wet day! Follow the track, branching off right at a gate just before a house **[SD888 673]** onto a grassy path. The path runs uphill alongside a drystone wall. Keep the wall on your left until you cross a stile next to a gate and bear right along an initially indistinct path, parallel to the road which you eventually cross **[SD884 691]** and take the track towards Tennant Gill Farm.

Small waterfall with Pen-y-Ghent in the background.

4. The track bears left past the farmyard and then straight ahead with a fence on the right hand side, with which it eventually converges. Cross a stile and then turn left (clearly marked Pennine Way). After a short distance turn right at another Pennine Way signpost and follow the line of an old stone wall and the old miners' track. At a corner of the old stone wall **[SD699 876]** you leave the old wall and head north-east and then northwards. The path climbs over Fountains Fell (2,191') and then down the other side to reach a road **[SD853 723]**.

Fountains Fell is named after the Cisterian monastery of Fountains Abbey. The path up Fountains Fell was originally a miner's track as there were extensive coal deposits underneath a millstone cap. Do not leave the path as there are disused mine shafts in the area.

5. On reaching the road turn left to cross over a cattle grid. Continue along the road to pass Rainscar House Farm and, just past some roadside parking, turn right **[SD843 714]** to pass Dale Head Farm. Pass Churn Milk Hole and then swing north towards Pen-y-Ghent. (Just before the ascent becomes really steep, in particularly adverse weather, you can take a shortcut down a path on the left hand side **[SD836 728]** which leads you to Bracken Bottom and into Horton-in-Ribblesdale.) Continue up the steep but unmistakeable path to the top.

Pen-y-Ghent.

48

Pen-y-Ghent translates (from Welsh!) as "hill of the winds" – aptly named as I have never been up there without it being windy. At 2,277' above sea level on a clear day it is possible to see Ingleborough and Whernside (the other two peaks of the famous Yorkshire 3 Peaks) as well as Pendle Hill, the Bowland Fells, the Howgills and Great Shunner Fell.

6. Cross the wall stile and follow the distinct path north-westwards and then westward down towards Horton-in-Ribblesdale. Eventually turn left onto the Bridleway [**SD823 743**], an old packhorse road, and at a fork turn right for a short distance into Horton-in-Ribblesdale. Turn right for the Pen-y-Ghent café [**SD808 725**].

Pen-y-Ghent cafe, Tel 01729 860333, is open until at least 6 pm every day. It is a real walkers' cafe and there is a register for those people who are on the Pennine Way. It is also the start and finish point for the Yorkshire 3 Peaks Challenge (www.thethreepeakschallenge.com), a challenging walk of 26 miles over Pen-y-Ghent, Whernside and Ingleborough. Finishing the walk within the 12 hours does give you a great sense of achievement and entitlement to join the 3 Peaks of Yorkshire Club.

DAY 5: HORTON-IN-RIBBLESDALE TO HAWES
Approaching Ling Gill Bridge.

DAY 5: HORTON-IN-RIBBLESDALE TO HAWES

Today's walk is classic fell-walking with open moorland, little shelter and few signs of habitation. The route is easy to find, as much of it is along green lanes, usually old packhorse routes. To aid navigation you are following the Ribble Way and then the Pennine Way. There are some excellent views, particularly of the Three Peaks of Yorkshire – especially emotive if you have ever completed the challenge.

The market town of Hawes is an excellent destination with a wide range of accommodation. The youth hostel (01969 667368) just west of the town centre is rather spartan (no hot water the night that I stopped). For bed and breakfast establishments Laburnum House (01969 667717) and the walker-friendly Herriott's Guest House, www.herriotsinhawes.co.uk, (01696 667536) are both central. There are also a large range of pubs which offer accommodation as well as excellent food and ale – my personal recommendation is Cockett's Hotel, www.cocketts.co.uk, (01969 667312). You should have no difficulty in finding accommodation, and all seem to offer packed lunches ready for the next day's walk.

Hawes has many shops, cafes and restaurants. There is also a laundrette open 9:30 am to 4:00 pm (closed Wednesdays and Sundays). The very interesting and informative Dales Countryside Museum is open 10am-5pm daily – somewhere to call before commencing tomorrow's relatively short walk.

There is a bus service from Hawes to Garsdale Station (http://getdown.org.uk/bus/bus/113.htm) from where you can catch a train to Leeds. Local taxi services can be contacted on 01969 667598 and 01969 650441 (the latter also offers a minibus service).

DISTANCE:	14 miles.
ASCENT:	1100'
TERRAIN:	Field paths and tracks.
TIME:	6 hours
START:	Horton-in-Ribblesdale
MAPS:	OL2 Yorkshire Dales Southern & Western

FGS Grading
Grading F6 [D2, N1, T1, R2, H0]

Distance	2	12-18 miles
Navigation	1	Basic navigation skills needed
Terrain	1	50-75% on graded track or path
Remoteness	2	Countryside not in close proximity to habitation – less than 20% of the route within 2 miles
Height gain	0	Less than 100 ft per mile

The wooded
slopes of
Ling Gill.

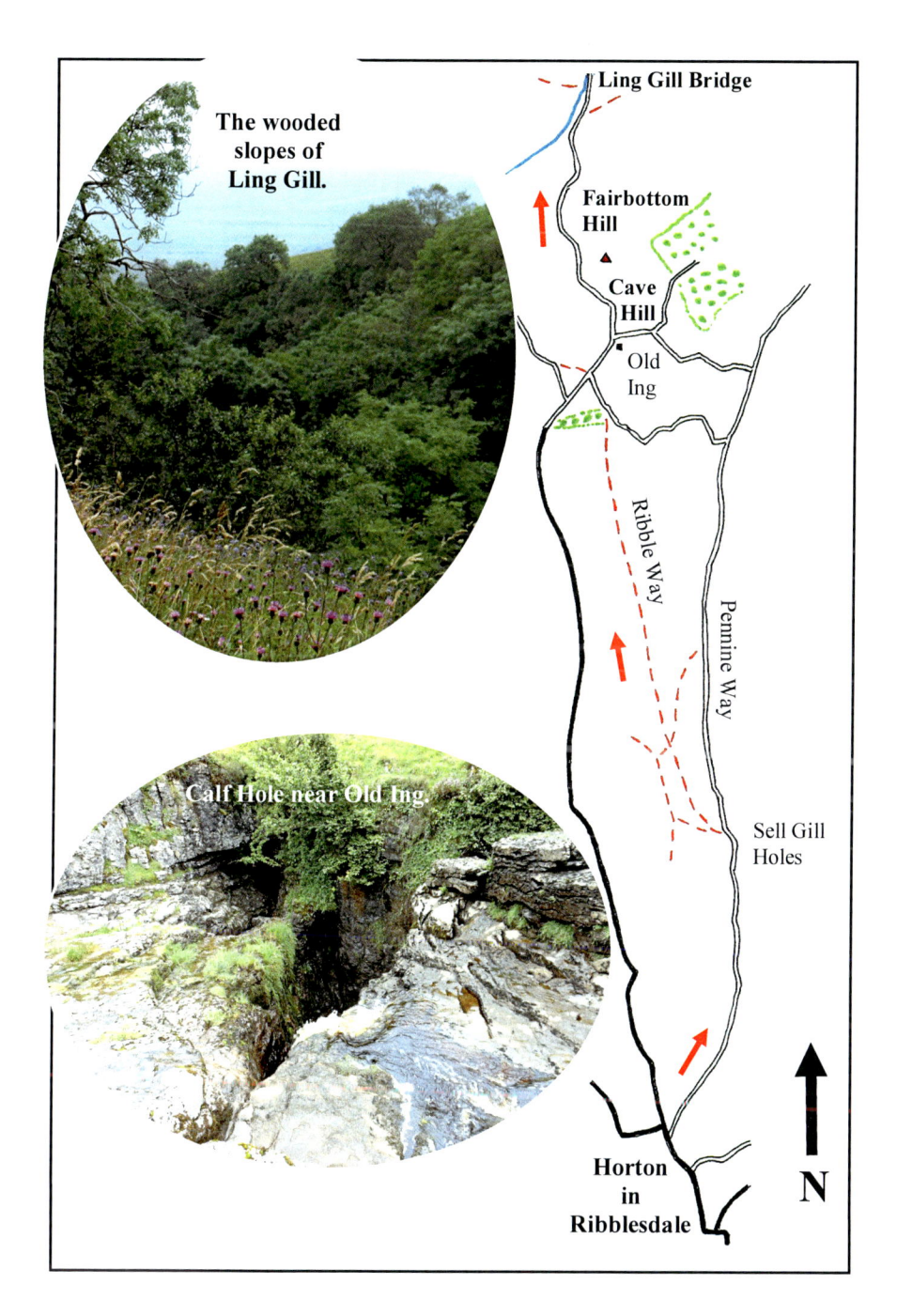

Ling Gill Bridge

Fairbottom
Hill

Cave
Hill

Old
Ing

Ribble Way

Pennine Way

Sell Gill
Holes

Calf Hole near Old Ing.

Horton
in
Ribblesdale

N

A distant Ribblehead Viaduct.

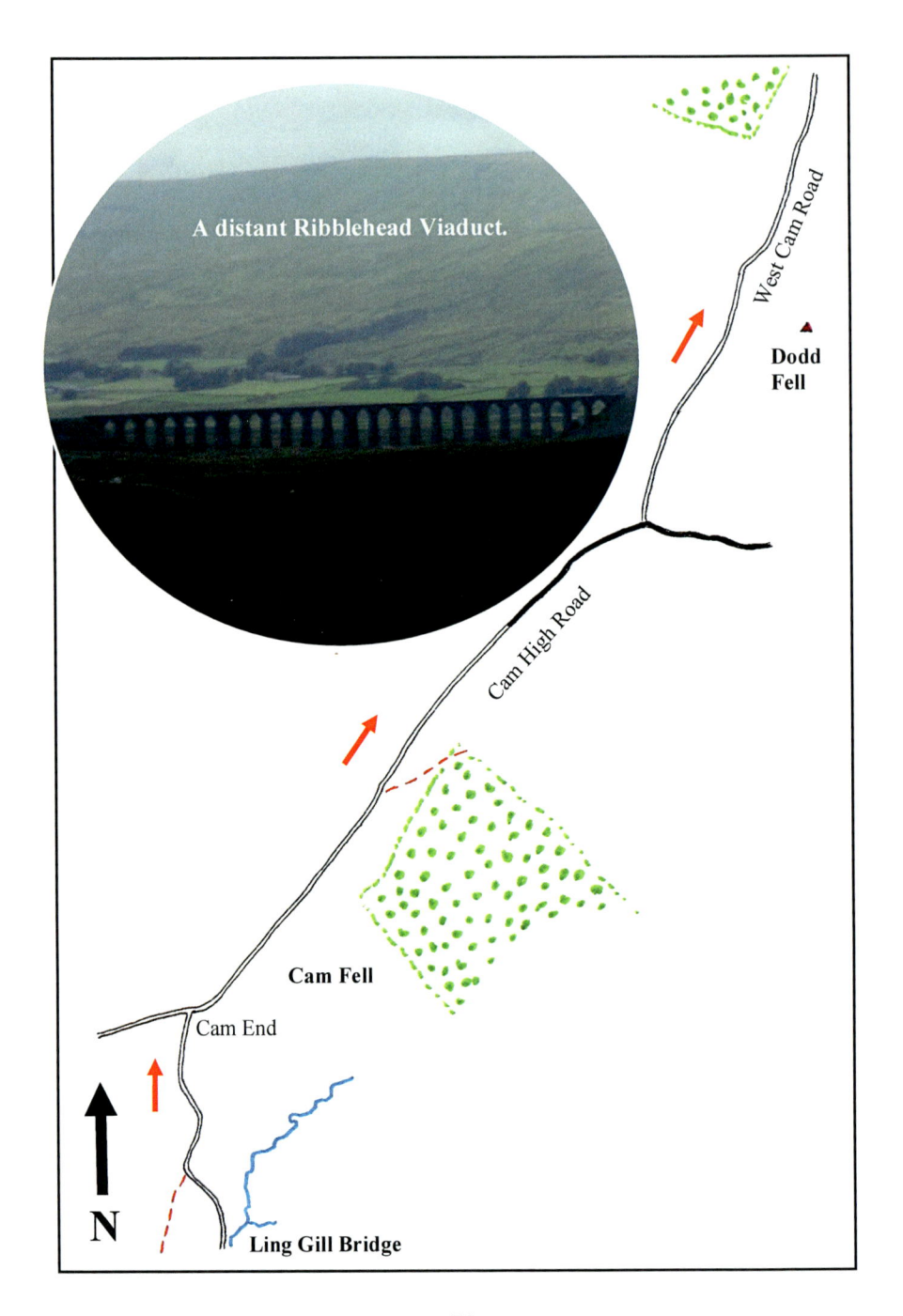

West Cam Road

▲ Dodd Fell

Cam High Road

Cam Fell

Cam End

N

Ling Gill Bridge

St Margaret's Church, Hawes.

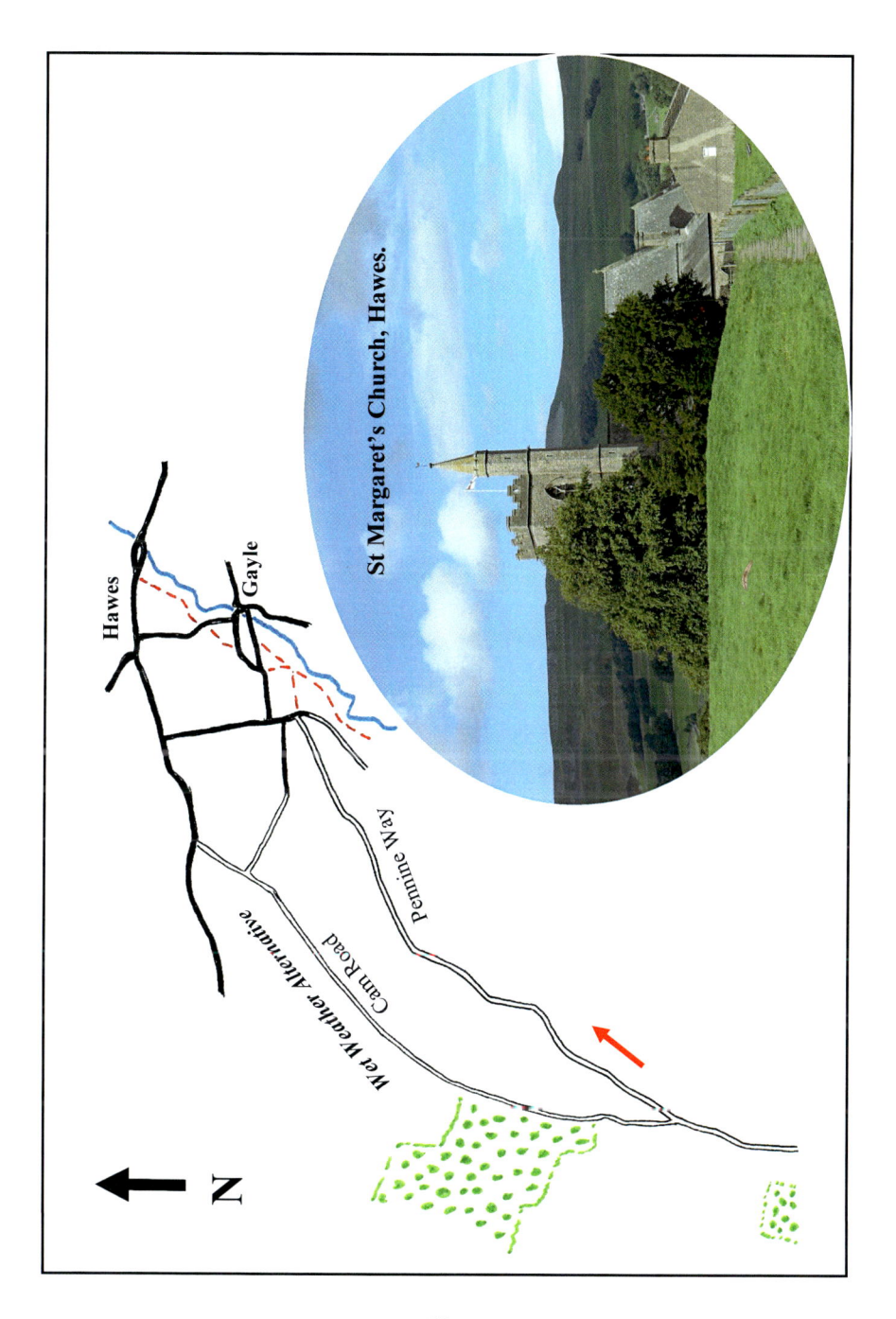

Hawes
Gayle
West Weather Alternative
Cam Road
Pennine Way
N

THE WALK

1. Continue through Horton, over the bridge and turn right into the Crown Inn car park **[SD808 727]**. Turn left onto Harbor Scar Lane, a stony walled track. Pass through a gate and continue to the highpoint of the climb. As the track swings right, pass through a smaller gate on the left hand side. Carry straight on keeping the stone wall on your left hand side to cross a stile (signposted Ribble Way) by a barn. Circle round the barn **[SD811 744]**, pass through a large metal gate and carry on beside the right hand wall. Maintain the same direction, passing through two fields, and then to the left of a low limestone escarpment. Ignore a path which forks off to the left. The path then continues in the same direction for some distance. Just before a wooded gulley bear right upwards, taking a higher course along the escarpment. Skirt round the fenced head of the wooded gulley and, joining a track, follow it left to pass through a gate. At a junction of tracks **[SD803 772]** turn right and after a short distance at another junction of tracks turn left.

This is the pre-turnpike pack horse route from Settle to Hawes. There is evidence that at least parts of the road could be Roman or earlier.

2. You are now following the Pennine Way again. This winds between Cave Hill and Fair Bottom Hill to reach the deep limestone ravine of Ling Gill and pass through Ling Gill National Nature Reserve. The route passes Ling Gill

Ling Gill Bridge

Bridge (5 miles) **[SD803 789]** and this is an idyllic place to pause for a break.

Ling Gill National Nature Reserve is a small sub-alpine woodland. It is situated in a narrow limestone gorge through which flows Cam Beck and contains Birch, Rowan and Ash trees along with rare plants. These survive because the steep slopes have prevented access to grazing animals.

Ling Gill Bridge was built in the 16th century and a commemorative stone built into the bridge marks its repair in 1765. Cam High Road was a Roman road which ran between the Roman fort at Bainbridge and Ingleton which followed the alignment of a prehistoric track. It was repaired as part of the Richmond to Lancaster Turnpike road but abandoned around 1795.

3. The trail now meanders uphill – look left to see views of the Ribblehead Viaduct. Continue to Cam End and turn right **[SD802 804]** to join the Dales Way along Cam High Road.

Ribblehead Viaduct, on the Settle to Carlisle railway, was opened in 1874. It has 24 arches, is 104' high and took 6,000 navvies to build it – hundreds of whom died in the process. If you ever get the chance you should visit Ribblehead Station and look at the fascinating exhibition of the railway's history.

4. The Dales Way forks off to the right, but the Pennine Way continues along the high top and eventually joins a tarmac track rising up from Camm Farm. Continue to Kidhow Gate (1,877' and 7.85 miles into today's walk). Fork left **[SD829 833]** off the road onto the old packhorse road, now called West Cam Road.

If you look left now you should be able to see all three of the famous 3 Peaks of Yorkshire - the gritstone capped peaks of Pen-y-Ghent, Whernside and Ingleborough. Also look left and marvel at the straightness of the dry stone walls which rise up on the far side of the valley of Snaizeholme.

5. Follow West Cam Road for approximately 45 minutes before you bear right onto a path signposted Pennine Way (11 miles into the walk) **[SD842 868]**. [In particularly wet weather, after a prolonged period of rain or failing light you should continue straight ahead to the end. Turn right onto the main road to walk into Hawes]. The path climbs up in roughly the same direction before dropping down and bearing right.

As you descend you look ahead into the fertile dale of Wensleydale (home to the cheese beloved by Wallace and Gromit!) www.wensleydale.org

Views across Wensleydale.

6. Pass Gaudy House on the left. Continue into Gaudy Lane, a tarmac track, and follow it to the end **[SD865 889]**. Turn right and then almost immediately left over two fields and then turn left (not bear left!) down to a lane. Turn right and then left down another lane **[SD868 891]**. Follow the lane down past Rookhurst Country House and bear left onto a flagged path which runs diagonally across two fields. Cross straight over a road and pass between houses. Cross straight over again to pass between more houses. Turn left onto a road, and then right along a flagged path above Gayle Beck to pass to the right of St Margaret's church and emerge opposite the White Hart in the centre of Hawes **[SD873 898]**.

The White Hart Inn (01969 667214) is an old coaching Inn and stage post dating from the late 16th century. Offers good ales, food and accommodation. www.whitehartcountryinn.co.uk

DAY 6: HAWES TO KELD
Passing one of the cairns on the descent from Great Shunner Fell.

DAY 6: HAWES TO KELD

As this is a relatively short walk I would recommend exploring Hawes before setting off late mid-morning. A particular recommendation is the Dales Countryside Museum (www.thedales.org.uk/DalesCountrysideMuseum), which is right on the route and open from 10am.

The walk follows the Pennine Way. It features a long, but invigorating, 5 mile climb up Great Shunner Fell taking you out of Wensleydale. The walk then drops down into Swaledale, pausing for refreshments in Thwaite. Continue through some lovely walking over the shoulder of Kisdon Hill and on to Keld. Keld is a small village in the Yorkshire Dales positioned at the head of Swaledale, which is a beautiful narrow valley following the river Swale down to Richmond.

Refreshments can be obtained at the Kearton Tea Shop in Thwaite – a very popular spot for walkers to pause.

Keld is where the Coast to Coast walk and the Pennine Way cross, accommodation is limited and you should book well in advance. Keld Lodge, Tel 01748 886259 (www.keldlodge.com) is my personal recommendation, having stopped there three times now – great food, real ale, good views and a drying room. Butt House, Tel 01784 886374 (www.butthousekeld.co.uk) also offers Bed & Breakfast accommodation. Should you fail to secure accommodation here you may wish to continue a further 4 miles to the Tan Hill Inn, Tel 01833 628246 (www.tanhillinn.com – you've got to visit this website!). Should you need, or wish, to carry on to the Tan Hill, there is a village shop, open till 6 pm, at Park House in Keld where you can stock up on provisions.

In Keld, the newly opened Keld Countryside and Heritage Centre is well worth a visit.

There is a limited bus service from Keld to Richmond.

DISTANCE: 13 miles.
ASCENT: 2481'
TERRAIN: Field paths and tracks.
TIME: 6 hours
START: Hawes
MAPS: OL30 Yorkshire Dales Northern and Central

FGS Grading
Grading F8 [D2, N1, T1, R2, H2]

Distance	2	12-18 miles
Navigation	1	Basic navigation skills needed
Terrain	1	50-75% on graded track or path
Remoteness	2	Countryside not in close proximity to habitation
Height gain	2	Over 125 ft per mile

Hearne Edge

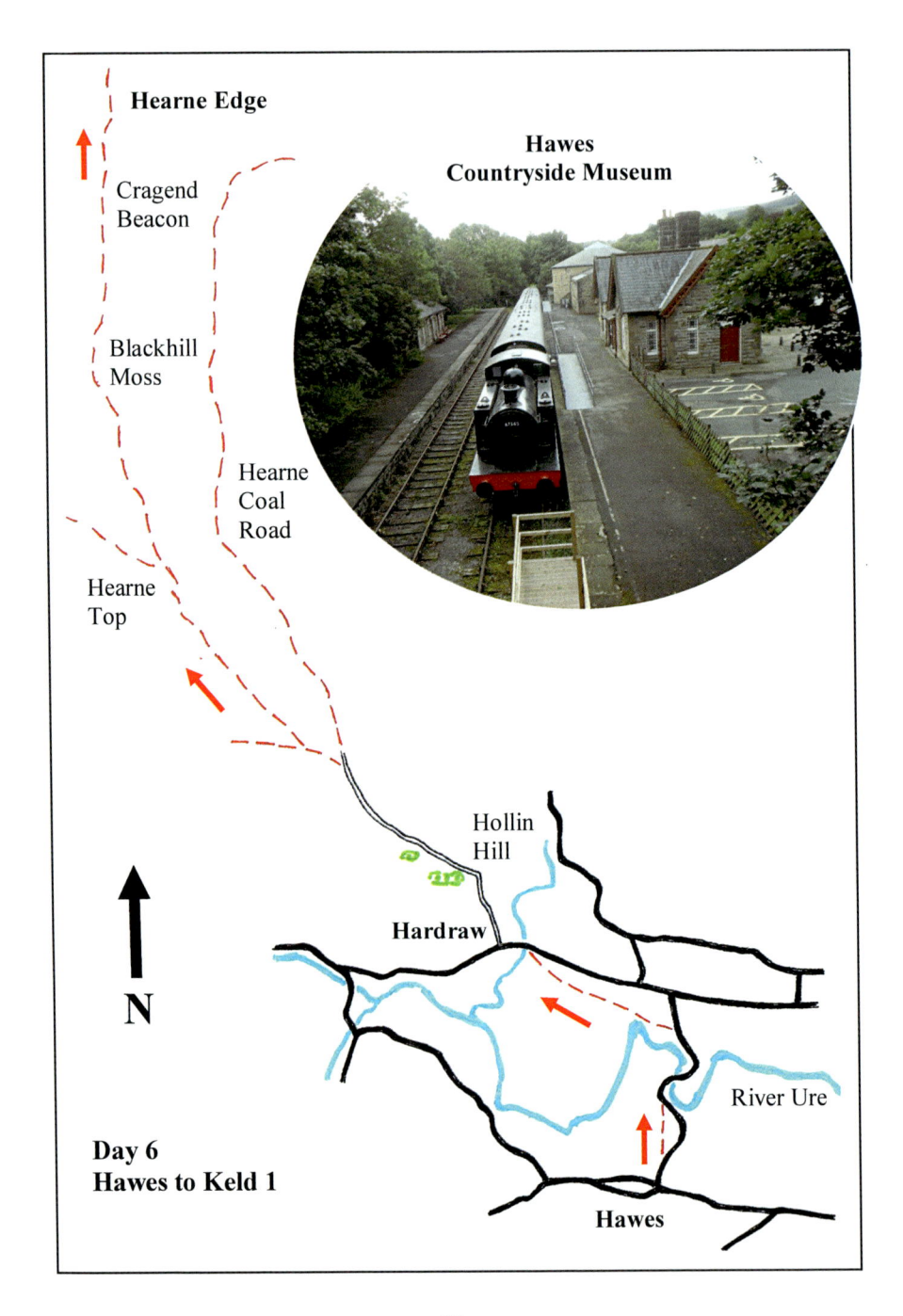

Cragend Beacon

Blackhill Moss

Hearne Coal Road

Hearne Top

Hawes Countryside Museum

Hollin Hill

Hardraw

River Ure

**Day 6
Hawes to Keld 1**

N

Hawes

Day 6 Hawes to Keld 2

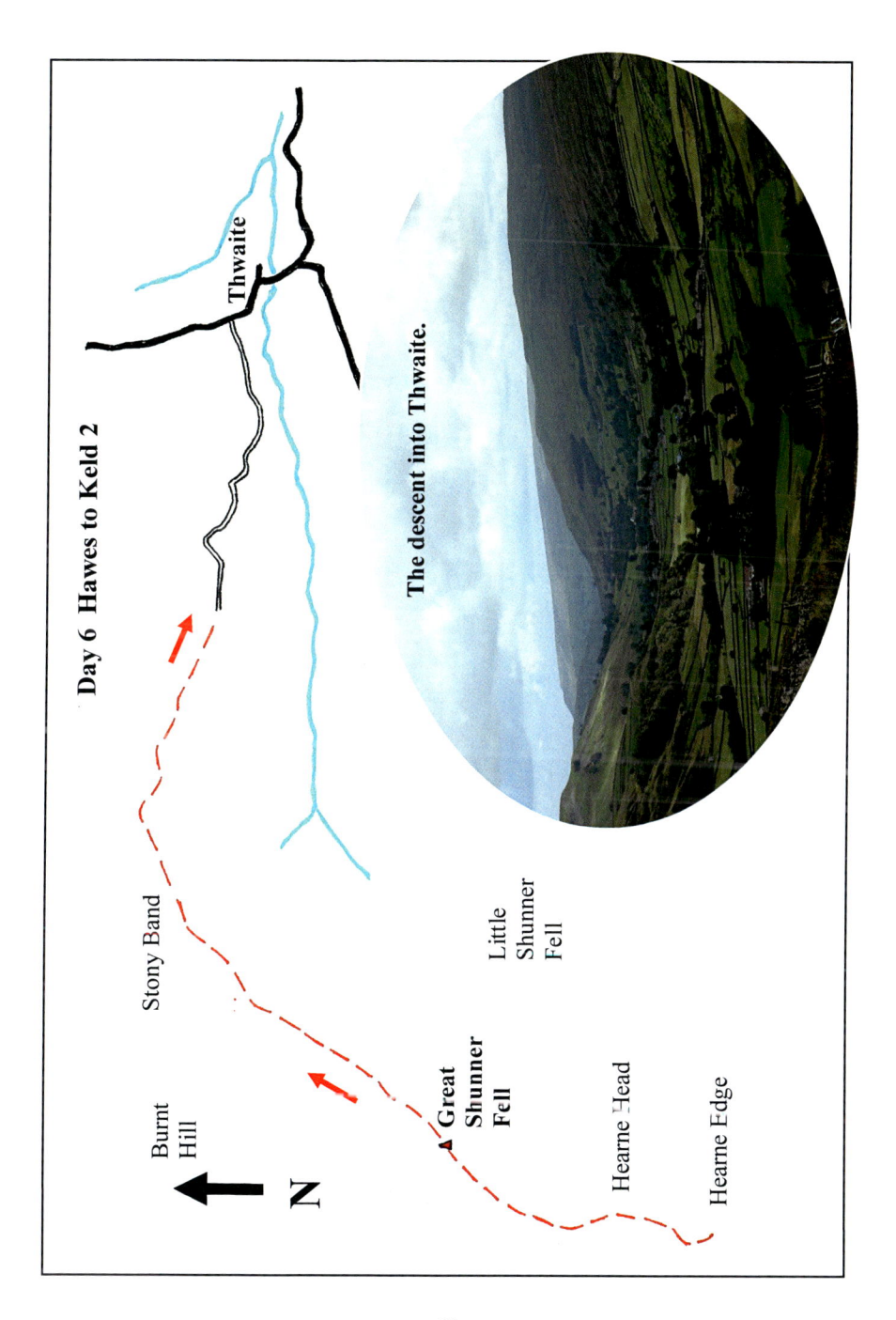

Thwaite

Stony Band

Burnt Hill

N

Great Shunner Fell

Little Shunner Fell

Hearne Head

Hearne Edge

The descent into Thwaite.

Looking down on the River Swale.

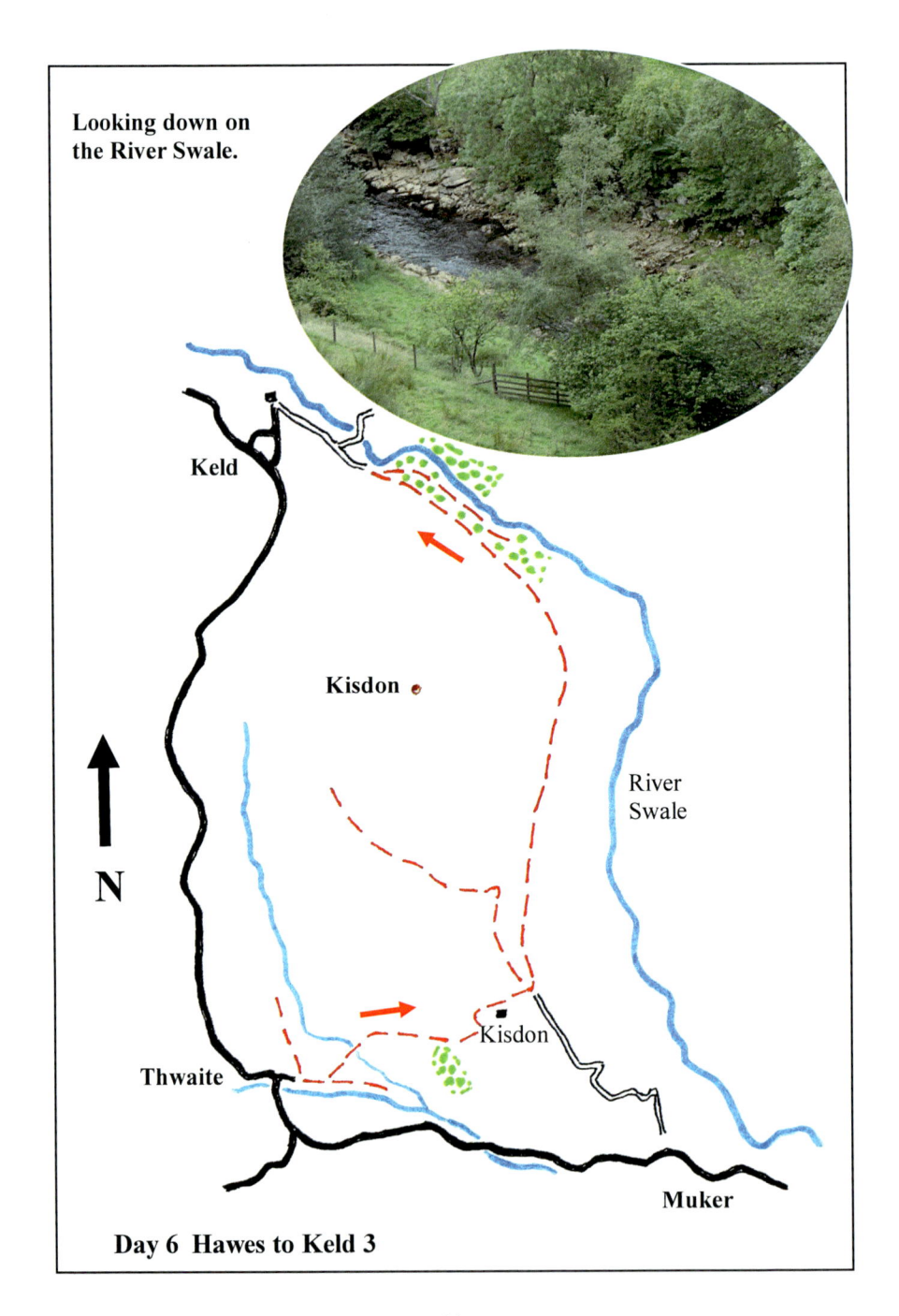

Keld

Kisdon

River Swale

Thwaite

Kisdon

Muker

N

Day 6 Hawes to Keld 3

THE WALK

1. From the east end of Hawes follow Brunt Acres Road north over the disused railway line **[SD875 899]** with the old railway station on the right hand side, also the Dales Countryside Museum. Cut a corner across the meadows on a path to return to the road. Cross Haylands Bridge then turn left on a waymarked path **[SD877 907]**, signposted Hardraw, across pastures linked by stiles. Turn left onto the road to cross Hardraw Bridge (just beyond Hardraw Force).

The climb up Great Shunner Fell is excellent but always windy. In extremely windy conditions, and as a last resort, follow these instructions: After crossing Haylands Bridge follow Brunt Acres Road to the end. Turn left and then turn right, bear left and follow the road. It is 5 miles of road walking and it has been described by Jeremy Clarkson as "England's only truly spectacular road"- look up Buttertubs Pass on YouTube!

Hardraw Force is England's biggest single drop at 100 foot. Access is by payment through the Green Dragon Pub. I have never visited but have been told twice that it's a bit of a disappointment.

2. Turn right immediately after a slate clad house **[SD866 912]** into a stone walled drove road, which climbs up Hollins Hill and then bears left, continuing to climb. Pass through a metal gate and bear left at a junction of tracks **[SD858 921]**. At Hearne Top bear right **[SD847 932]** as the track heads in a more northerly direction. The track continues for 5 miles up Great Shunner Fell, over several false summits, until it finally reaches the summit (2,384') just beyond

The path leading away from the summit shelter on Great Shunner Fell.

Crag End Beacon.

Moorland birds are prolific here, lapwings, golden plovers, grouse, curlews, dunlin, sanderlings and numerous skylarks.

3. After a rest in the wind shelter the track now heads north-eastwards across a fence towards Beacon Cairn. The path drops steeply past succesive cairns and then curves round to run alongside Thwaite Beck, to eventually enter another stony drove road and then turn right onto the road into Thwaite.

The descent down into Thwaite.

Thwaite derives from the Norse name for a clearing in the forest. In prehistoric times England was largely covered with woodland. By the end of the first millennium much had already been cleared to satisfy the needs of an increasing population. This area would have been covered with either oak woods or hazel woods.

4. After refreshments at the Kearton Tea Shop **[SD892 982]** continue east along the side street into a footpath and from a stile follow the field path north eastwards towards Kisdon Hill. Pass through two large metal gates then diagonally right to the top corner. The path contours round Kisdon Hill. Take care to follow the PW signs, especially easy to miss is the bear left through a wooden

Heading towards Keld and, inset, a blockage in the path.

gate at Kisdon House. The path is clear but is stony scree, which is difficult in wet weather, until it angles downhill through woods opposite Kisdon Force and on into Keld **[NY893 012]**.

Force comes from the Norse word fors or foss, which means "waterfall". The name Keld derives from the Viking word Kelda, meaning "a spring".

DAY 7: KELD TO BALDERSDALE
East Gill Force, passed after leaving Keld.

DAY 7: KELD TO BALDERSDALE

Today's walk mostly features moorland walking, the big skies, the solitude and the cry of the moorland birds. Along the way you also encounter the historic Tan Hill Inn, the remnants of long abandoned collieries and God's Bridge. This has been described by Natural England as the best example of a natural limestone bridge in the country. There are no refreshments available but God's Bridge is an excellent place to pause and eat your packed lunch. If the weather is particularly inclement there is a large new wooden shelter after you cross Ravock Moor and just before you cross Deepdale Beck.

Today's destination is set in spectacular scenery at the head of Baldersdale in an area of outstanding natural beauty. Accommodation is either the Youth Hostel at Baldersdale or Clove Lodge. The Youth Hostel according to the YHA website is "only available at weekends and in school holidays for exclusive use groups". Clove Lodge, on the other hand, I can assure you from personal experience offers exceptional hospitality and home cooked meals. As this is the only accommodation in the area advanced booking is almost certainly essential. Details can be found on the website at www.thepennineway.co.uk/clovelodge, Tel 01833 650030.

If you arrive early you can explore the adjacent reservoir of Blackton. This is a haven for wildlife with a local nature reserve and a large modern bird hide.

Postscript.
On my last visit to Clove Lodge (August 2012) it was up for sale. If Clove Lodge is no longer a bed and breakfast then the best alternative that I can think of is as follows. Day 6 Hawes to Tan Hill pub. Day 7 Tan Hill to Middleton-in-Teesdale. Day 8 Middleton-in-Teesdale to Langdon Beck.

DISTANCE:	15 miles.
ASCENT:	1,260'
TERRAIN:	Field paths and tracks.
TIME:	7 hours
START:	Keld
MAPS:	OL30 Yorkshire Dales Northern and Central
	OL31 North Pennines Teesdale and Weardale

FGS Grading
Grading F7 [D2, N1, T1, R2, H1]

Distance	2	12-18 miles
Navigation	1	Basic navigation skills needed
Terrain	1	50-75% on graded track or path
Remoteness	2	Countryside not in close proximity to habitation
Height gain	1	Less than 100 ft per mile

Day 7
Keld to Baldersdale 1

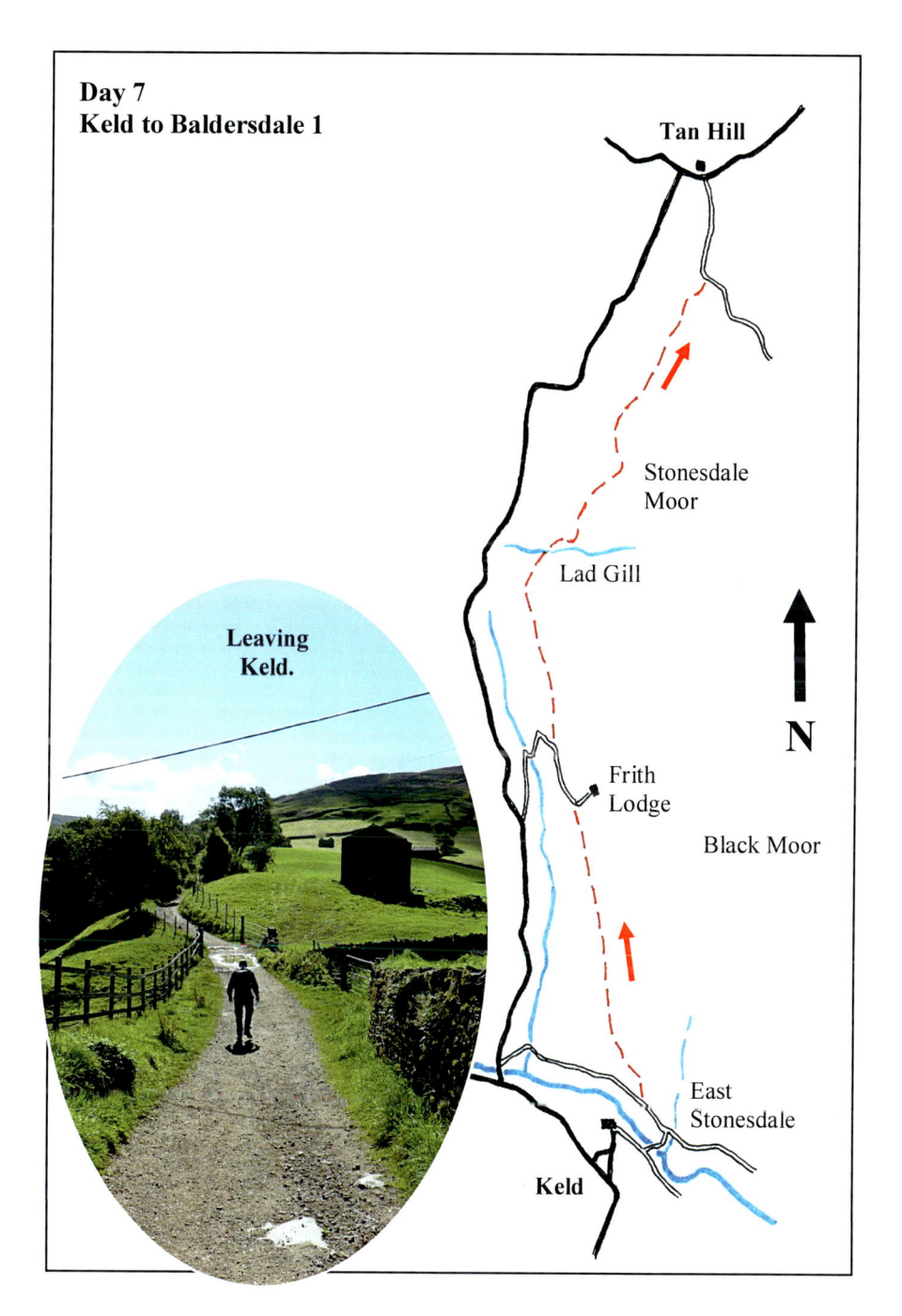

Tan Hill

Stonesdale Moor

Lad Gill

Frith Lodge

Black Moor

N

Leaving Keld.

East Stonesdale

Keld

71

The Sleightholme Beck.

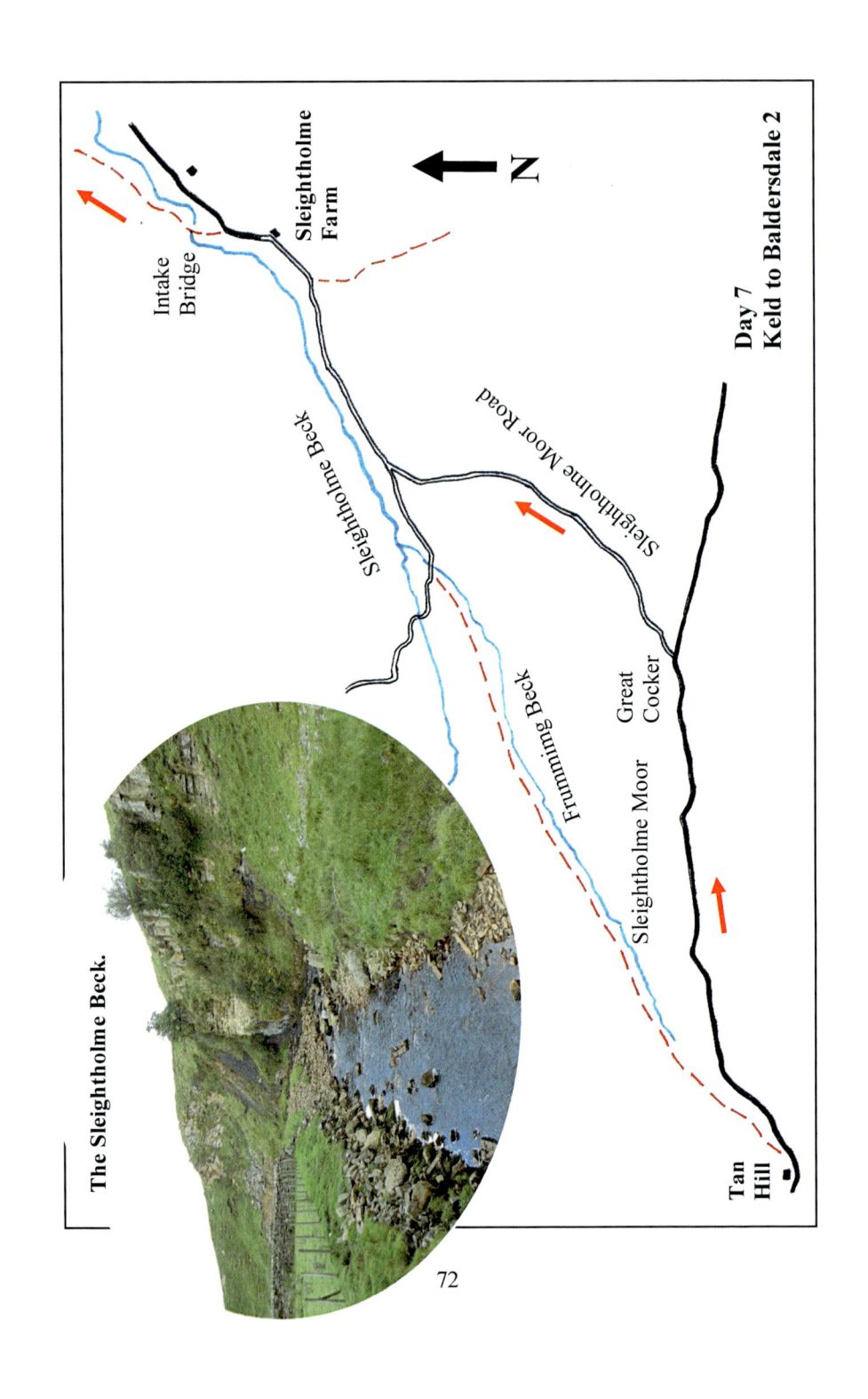

Day 7
Keld to Baldersdale 2

N

Sleightholme Farm
Intake Bridge
Sleightholme Beck
Frumming Beck
Sleightholme Moor Road
Great Cocker
Sleightholme Moor
Tan Hill

Ravock

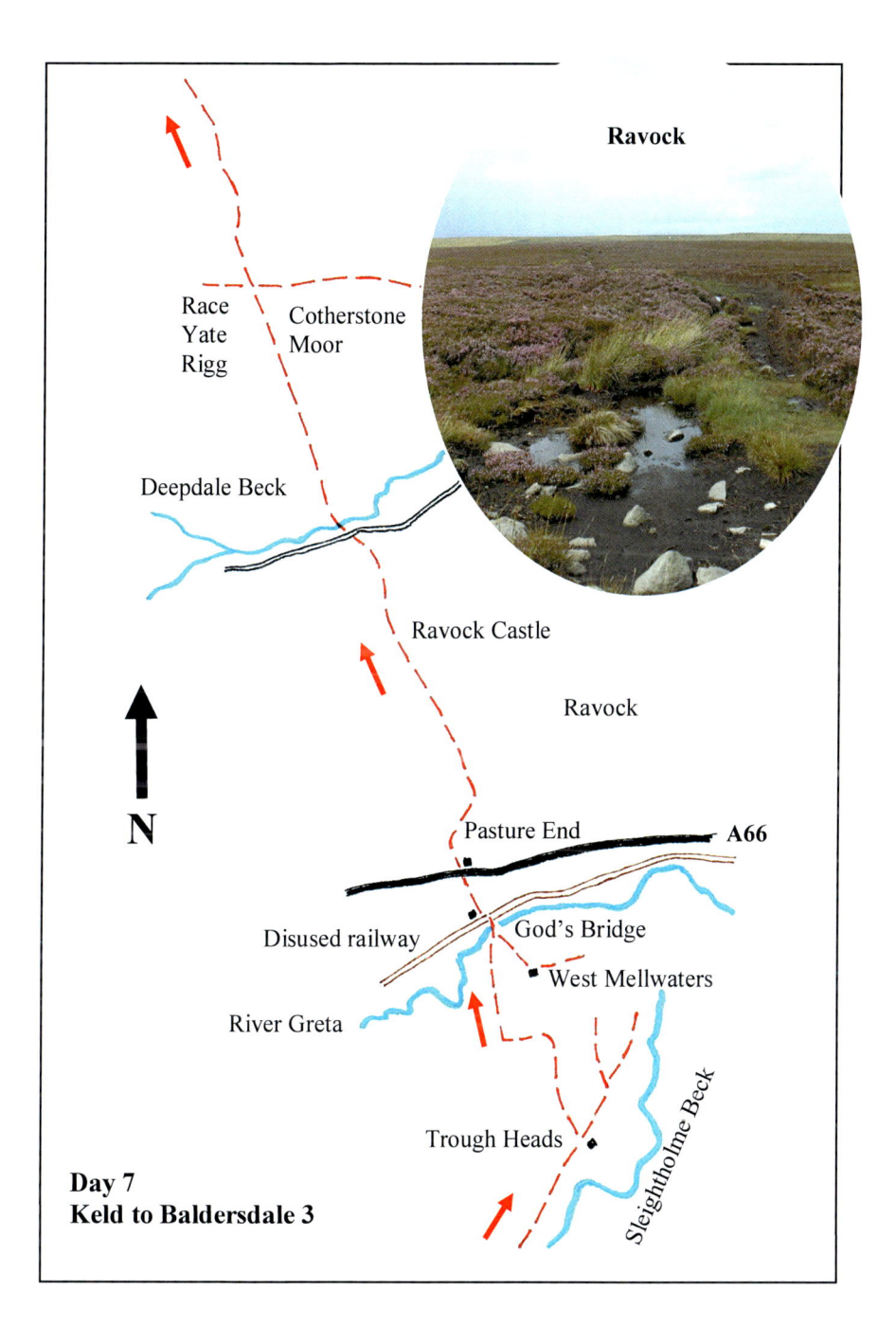

Race Yate Rigg
Cotherstone Moor

Deepdale Beck

Ravock Castle

Ravock

N

Pasture End — A66
Disused railway
God's Bridge
West Mellwaters
River Greta

Trough Heads

Sleightholme Beck

Day 7
Keld to Baldersdale 3

Day 7
Keld to Baldersdale 4

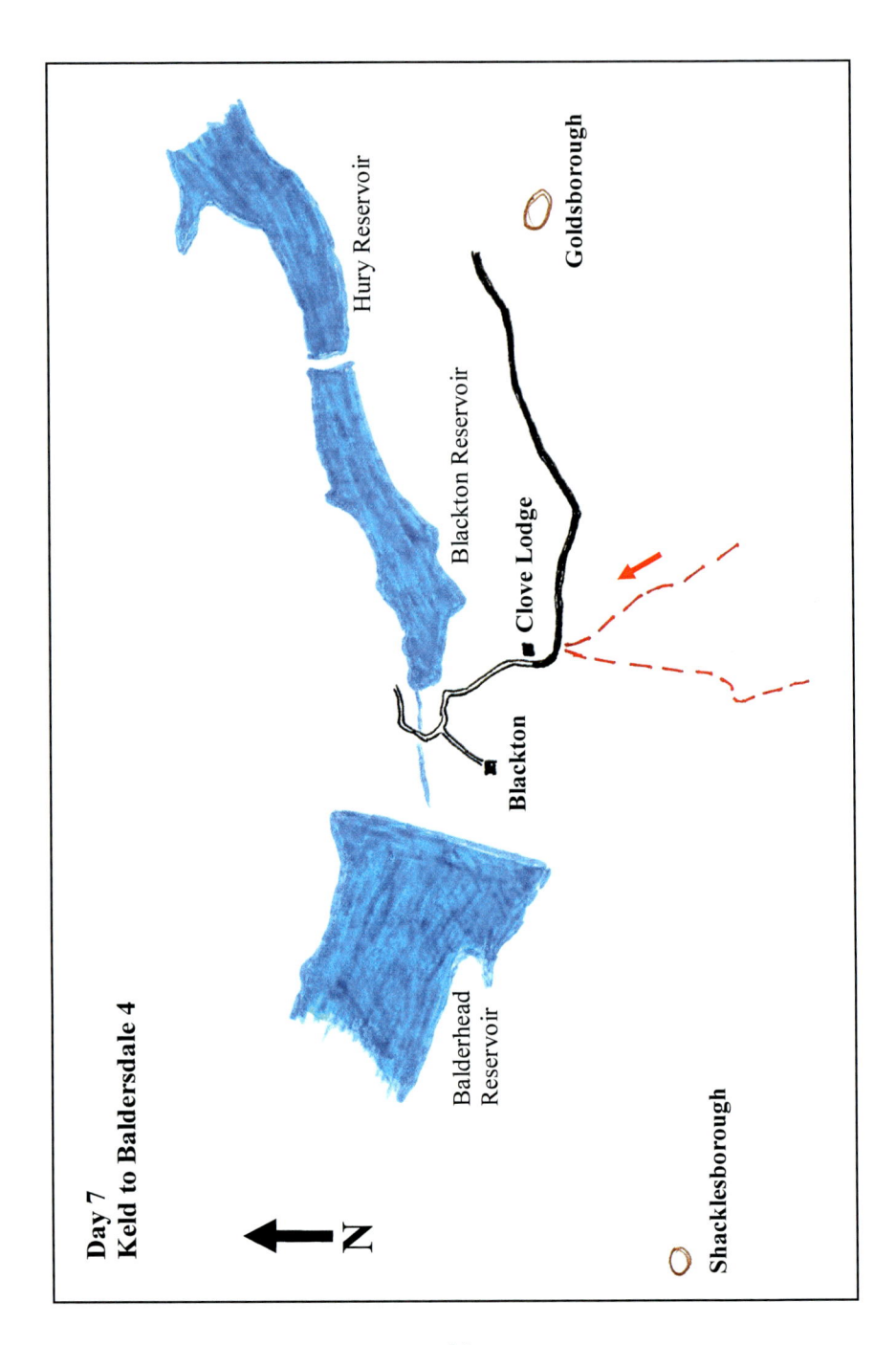

THE WALK

1. Turn back and then turn left across the footbridge over the Swale **[NY896 011]**. Turn left then bear right and then turn left up a steep track past East Stonesdale Farm (where the C2C walk crosses your route). Carry straight on through a wooden farm gate onto the old grassy road. Bear left at a barn. The route runs roughly parallel to a minor road before the cairned track veers north eastwards up Lad Gill to finally reach the Tan Hill pub (4 miles) **[NY897 067]**.

The Tan Hill Inn at 1,732' above sea level is Great Britain's highest pub. Historically this was the meeting point of 4 packhorse routes. It also served the needs of the many nearby, now derelict, collieries.

Approaching Tan Hill Inn and, inset, the signpost at the entrance to the Sleightholme Moor Road.

2. Turn right at the Tan Hill Inn, temporarily ignoring the Pennine Way signs, and follow the Arkengarthdale road eastwards for 2 miles. Fork left at Great Cocker **[NY929 075]** to follow the Sleightholme Moor Road track. Bear right onto the Pennine Way track which becomes a metalled track past Sleightholme Farm. Just after Kingdom Lodge fork left **[NY956 104]** to a wooden gate and then diagonally right to cross Sleightholme Beck via Intake Bridge. Follow the higher of the two tracks which rises up above and then follows the beck.

3. At Trough Heads Farm **[NY962 114]** fork North/North Westwards over moorland. Follow a line of white topped posts to the last post before the wall then turn left onto a barely visible bridleway which runs parallel to the wall. Cross a stream then turn right through a small wooden gate **[NY958 119]**. Follow the wall on the right hand side to cross the River Greta at God's Bridge **[NY957 126]**.

The limestone span of God's Bridge.

4. Cut through a dismantled railway and up a track. Turn left to pass through an underpass under the A66. Walk towards Pasture End house and then turn left uphill beside a wall. Bear right and then bear left towards a cairn **[NY954 138]**. The path over Ravock Moor is marked by piles of stones and eventually leads to a well-maintained wooden shelter (13 miles). Take the footbridge **[NY948 148]** over Deepdale Beck and through a gate to follow the drystone wall over several false summits to Race Yate Rigg (1,402'). Continue in the same direction over Cotherstone Moor to cross a footbridge **[NY941 165]**. The path is unclear but keep in a north-north-westerly direction until you reach a road **[NY936 176]**. Turn left onto the road to Clove Lodge.

Approaching Clove Lodge.

DAY 8: BALDERSDALE TO LANGDON BECK
High Force.

DAY 8: BALDERSDALE TO LANGDON BECK

This is a very pleasant day's walking. Starting past Blackton Reservoir and-Local Nature Reserve, the route climbs out of Baldersdale and then down into Lunedale. The path is initially across fields, climbing Harter Fell and across moorland to drop down towards Middleton-in-Teesdale – 7 miles into the walk, so almost halfway and an ideal spot to take a break.

There then follows a walk alongside the spectacular River Tees, one of my all-time favorite walks. This is a bird spotter's paradise with dippers, wagtails, sandpipers, goosanders, willow warblers, blackcaps, redstarts, oystercatchers and redshanks. This section also includes the impressive waterfalls of Low Force and the mighty High Force.

There are plenty of places for refreshments in Middleton-in-Teesdale – from personal experience I can recommend the Conduit Tea Rooms on the left hand side as you walk in, very walker friendly.

Accommodation is available at the Langdon Beck Youth Hostel, Tel 01833 622 228 (www.yha.org.uk), which has made a big effort to be environmentally friendly – rather spartan, but good food and fellow-walkers to chat to. Next to the youth hostel, if you prefer farmhouse hospitality, is East Under Hurth Farm B&B, Tel 01833 622062. East Under Hurth Farm is a working farm. Very reasonable rates. Emma and Michael are very welcoming, Emma does an excellent evening meal - and there's a bath! Just over a mile up the road (but bearing in mind you have already walked 15 miles ...) is the Langdon Beck Hotel, Tel 01833 622267 (www.langdonbeckhotel.com).

DISTANCE:	15.5 miles.
ASCENT:	2,050'
TERRAIN:	Field and riverside paths and tracks.
TIME:	8 hours
START:	Baldersdale
MAPS:	OL31 North Pennines Teesdale and Weardale

FGS Grading
Grading F7 [D2, N1, T1, R1, H2]

Distance	2	12-18 miles
Navigation	1	Basic navigation skills needed
Terrain	1	50-75% on graded track or path
Remoteness	1	Countryside in fairly close proximity to habitation
Height gain	2	Over 125 ft per mile

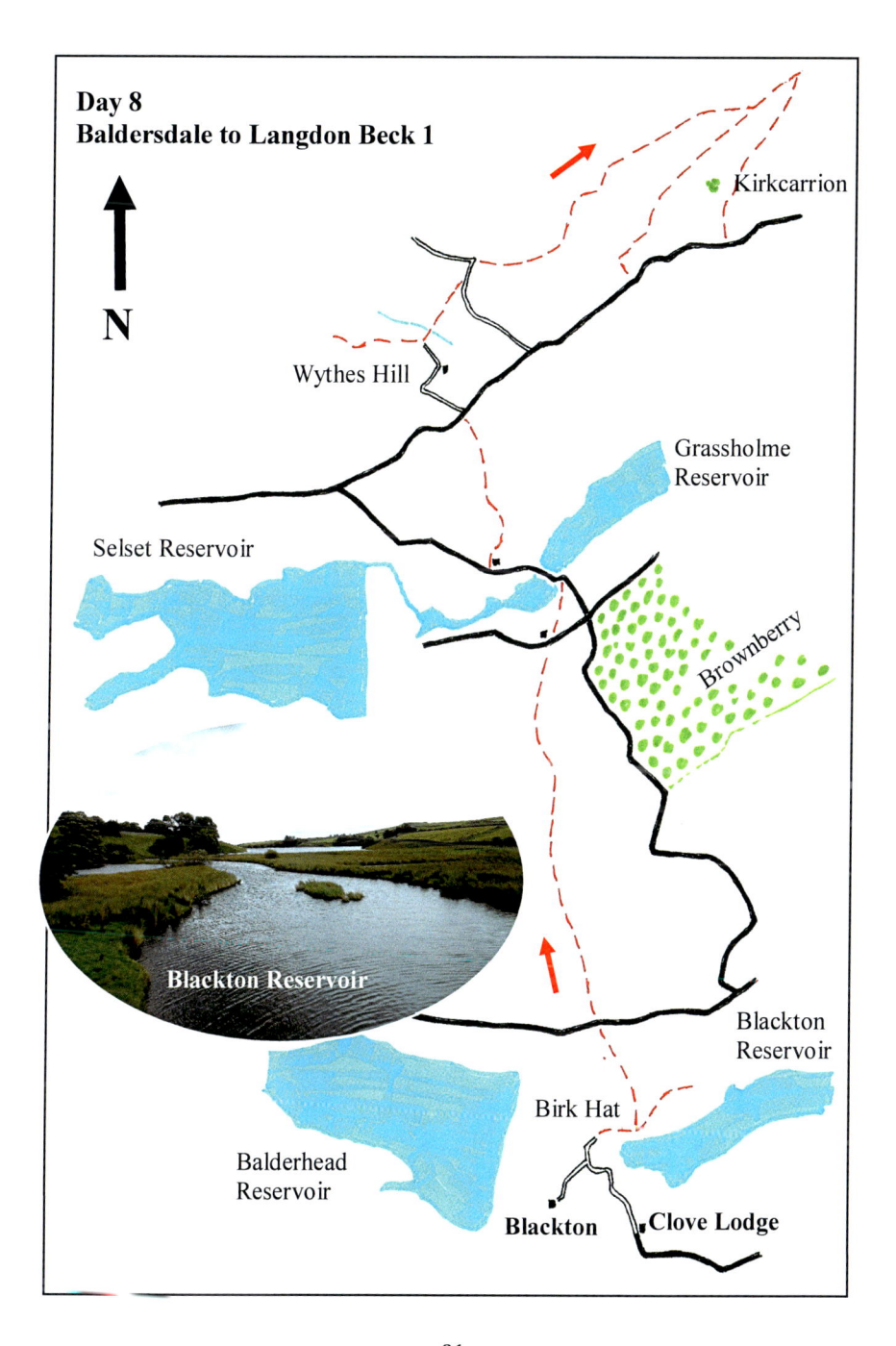

Day 8
Baldersdale to Langdon Beck 1

N

Kirkcarrion

Wythes Hill

Grassholme Reservoir

Selset Reservoir

Brownberry

Blackton Reservoir

Blackton Reservoir

Balderhead Reservoir

Birk Hat

Blackton Clove Lodge

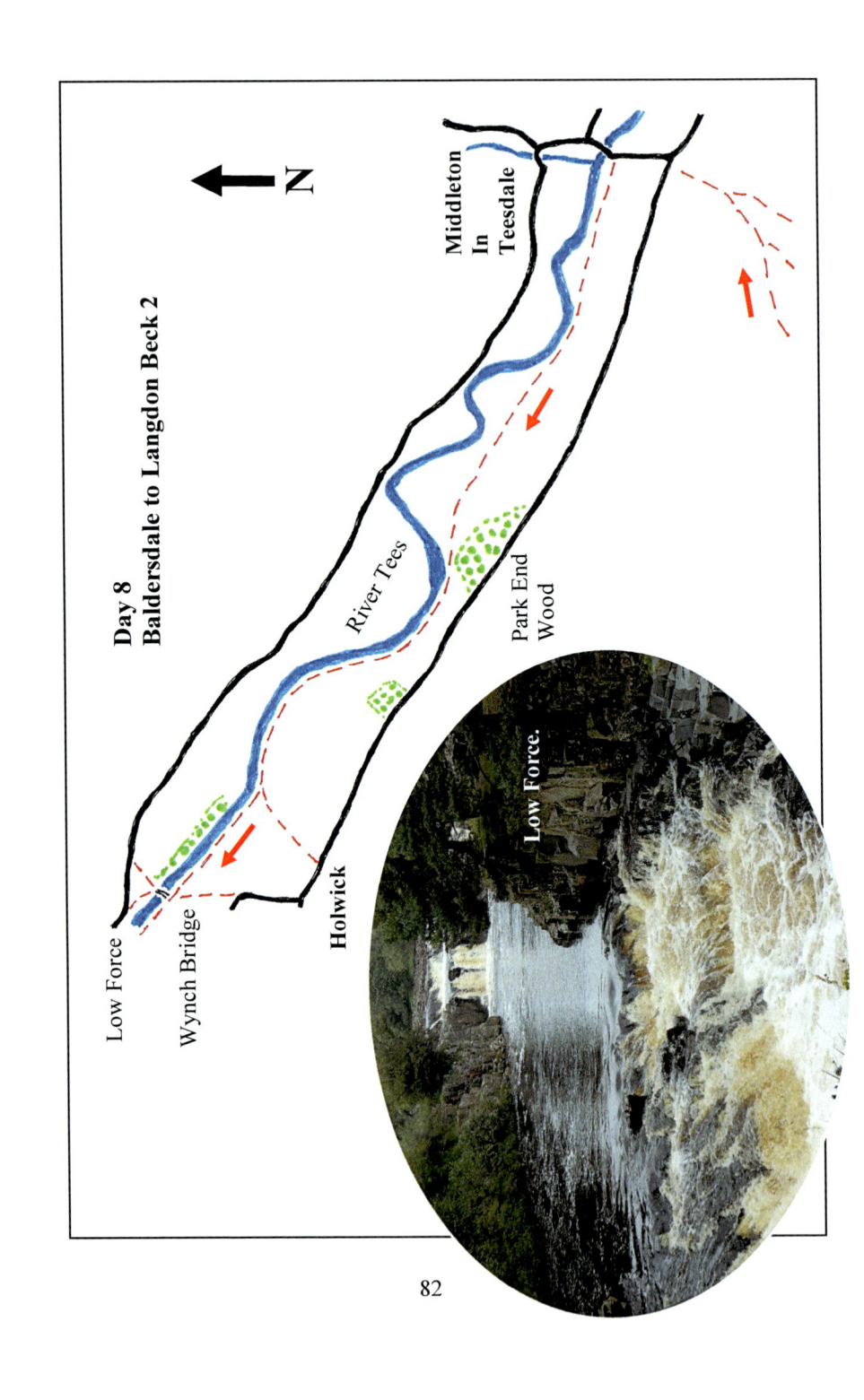

Day 8
Baldersdale to Langdon Beck 2

Middleton In Teesdale

River Tees

Park End Wood

Low Force

Wynch Bridge

Holwick

Low Force.

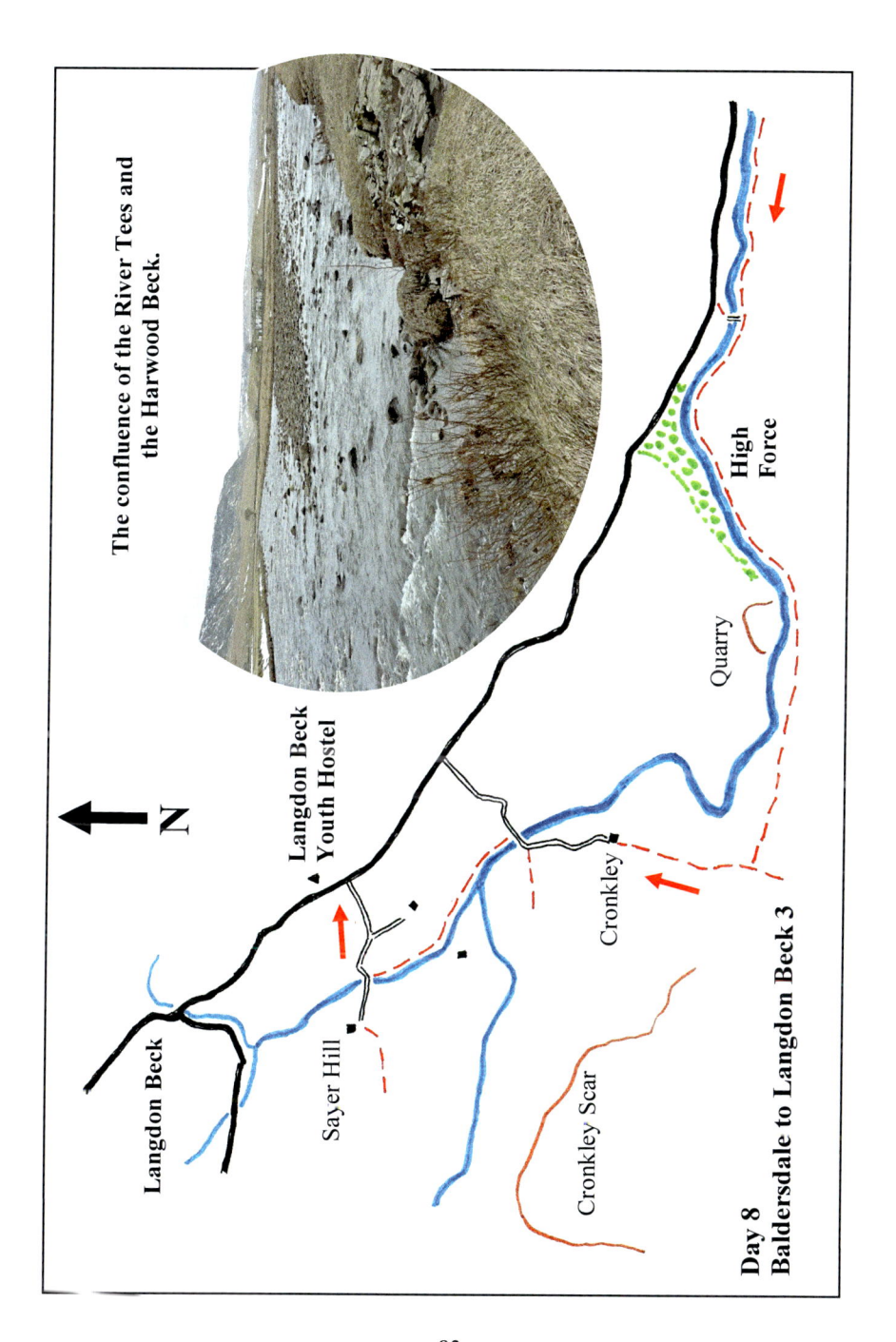

The confluence of the River Tees and the Harwood Beck.

N

Langdon Beck

Sayer Hill

Langdon Beck Youth Hostel

Cronkley

Cronkley Scar

Quarry

High Force

Day 8
Baldersdale to Langdon Beck 3

THE WALK

1. Crossing Blackton Bridge the track climbs eastwards through Blackton Nature Reserve to Birk Hat. Turn left up through pastureland past High Birk Hatt to a road **[NY933 190]**.

Blackton Nature Reserve is visited by several species of wader, especially the common sandpiper and gatherings of mallard, wigeon and tufted duck with whooper swan, wild geese and teal as occasional winter visitors. Birk Hat was for many years the home of Hannah Hauxwell, whose primitive life style made her a TV celebrity in 1973. "Hannah's Meadows" are owned by the Durham Wildlife Trust and kept as a site of Special Scientific Interest.

2. Turn left onto the road and then right and continue uphill. Follow the clear, if somewhat muddy, path until you cross two stiles in quick succession. After crossing the second stile turn left. At the end of the field the path moves away from the wall and heads for Beck Head farm buildings. The path then continues diagonally across fields to to the road **[NY930 212]**. Turn right onto the road and then left around the back of the house to drop down to Grassholme reservoir.

Grassholme reservoir is home to over 900 breeding pairs of black-headed gulls. A colony of jackdaws nests in disused rabbit burrows. There are also wigeon, snipe, oystercatcher and lapwing. Mammals include rabbit, water vole and short-tailed vole.

Grassholme Reservoir.

3. Cross the bridge over the reservoir and then follow the road to Grassholme Farm. Pass through the farmyard and continue northwards along the clearly marked path. The path passes through a number of meadows to a road. Cross the road onto the track up to Wythes Hill farm **[NY992 227]**. At the farm bear left down a walled track, across a stream and through a gate. Bear right to a stile and continue diagonally through another stile to reach a gateway at a junction of tracks. Go through the gateway and then turn right to follow the track through another gate. Continue to a stile by a barn **[NY926 233]**. Pass to the left of the barn and continue through another gateway and contour around Harter Fell. Pass through several fields.

If you look to the right you will see a clump of pine trees on a raised mound. This is Kirkcarrion, a Bronze Age burial site – no footpaths go near it!

4. Continue by dropping down to a well-marked grassy path which heads towards Middleton-in-Teesdale. The path continues to a gate in the corner, then down over a dismantled railway track **[NY946 248]**. Turn right and then left over the bridge into Middleton and the personally recommended Conduit Tea Rooms on the left hand side.

Middleton is a picturesque market town with excellent amenities. It was originally the site of a Saxon settlement. In the 19th century it expanded rapidly when it became the headquarters for the Quaker owned London Lead Company.

The River Tees at Middleton-in-Teesdale.

Following the River Tees towards High Force.

5. Turn back over the bridge and turn right **[NY946 251]** onto the path on the south bank of the Tees. Continue with the Tees to the right and Whin Sill to the left. The way eventually drops down to the river side and enters Moor House-Upper Teesdale National Nature Reserve. Continuing the walk you pass Low Force waterfall and then High Force waterfall **[NY880 283]**.

Whin Sill is a ribbon of volanic quartz-dolerite formed 295 million years ago which runs right across Northern England. The nature reserve is one of England's largest. It is particularly well known for the plants that originally colonised the high Pennines after the last ice age. You can also see rare rock formations such as sugar limestone. High Force has England's biggest single drop of 69 feet and, in my opinion, the most impressive waterfall you will encounter on this walk.

6. The path continues out of the woodland and continues upstream over the contour of Bracken Rigg then bears right to a stile.

The Tees from Bracken Rigg and, inset, one of the stone waymarkers from the top of the Rigg.

Continue alongside a wall to another stile and then down a gulley to Cronkley Farm **[NY862 289]**. The track heads north to cross a bridge

Heading down to Cronkley Farm.

then left along the other bank of the Tees. Continue alongside the river and, at a footbridge **[NY855 302]** over the Tees, turn right up a track and then left to the end and left onto the B6277. Langley Beck Youth Hostel is on the right hand side **[NY860 305]**. Langdon Beck Hotel is just over a mile further along.

DAY 9: LANGDON BECK TO DUFTON
Cauldron Snout

DAY 9: LANGDON BECK TO DUFTON

The first part of today's walk continues up the Tees, a rocky scramble over boulders and scree in places. The boulders have become polished and are a hazard in wet weather – do not underestimate how dangerous this can be if great care is not taken. On the plus side the scenery is wild and dramatic and you will almost certainly see kestrels, and possibly peregrines and merlins. This section of the walk ends in a dramatic climax when you climb up alongside Cauldron Snout to look out over Cow Green reservoir. The walk now follows farm roads and paths through remote, increasingly featureless, moorland until you suddenly reach High Cup Nick. With its sheer whinstone cliffs either side of a glacial valley, this is one of the absolute highlights of the whole walk, particularly the first time you see it. It was described by Wainwright as an 'unforgettable sight' - 'a natural wonder'. There are no refreshments available on the route so a packed lunch and drink is essential.

Dufton is a lovely little village with its own, very neat, website at **www.duftonvillage.info**. The Stag Inn, Tel: 017683 51608, (www.thestagdufton.co.uk) is walker friendly and everything a pub should be - oak beams, open fire, friendly barmaid, real ale and good food. Accommodation at Dufton comes in the form of yet another youth hostel, which is virtually opposite The Stag, Tel 0845 371 9734 (www.yha.org.uk). Farmhouse B&B can be obtained at Brow Farm, which you pass on the way into Dufton, Tel 017683 52582 (www.browfarm.com). On the other side of the village is Coneygarth B&B, Tel 017683 52582 (www.coneygarth.co.uk). Coneygarth can provide you with a good packed lunch, but if you venture to The Stag make sure you take a torch to find your way back!

DISTANCE:	14 miles.
ASCENT:	1,610'
TERRAIN:	Paths, muddy or boggy in places, tracks and rocky scrambles/climb.
TIME:	8 hours
START:	Langdon Beck
MAPS:	OL31 North Pennines Teesdale and Weardale
	OL19 Howgill Fells and Upper Eden Valley

FGS Grading
Grading F8 [D2, N1, T2, R2, H1]

Distance	2	12-18 miles
Navigation	1	Basic navigation skills needed
Terrain	2	25-50% on graded track or path
Remoteness	2	Countryside not in close proximity to habitation – less than 20% of the route within 2 miles
Height gain	1	Over 100 ft per mile

Day 9
Langdon Beck to Dufton 1

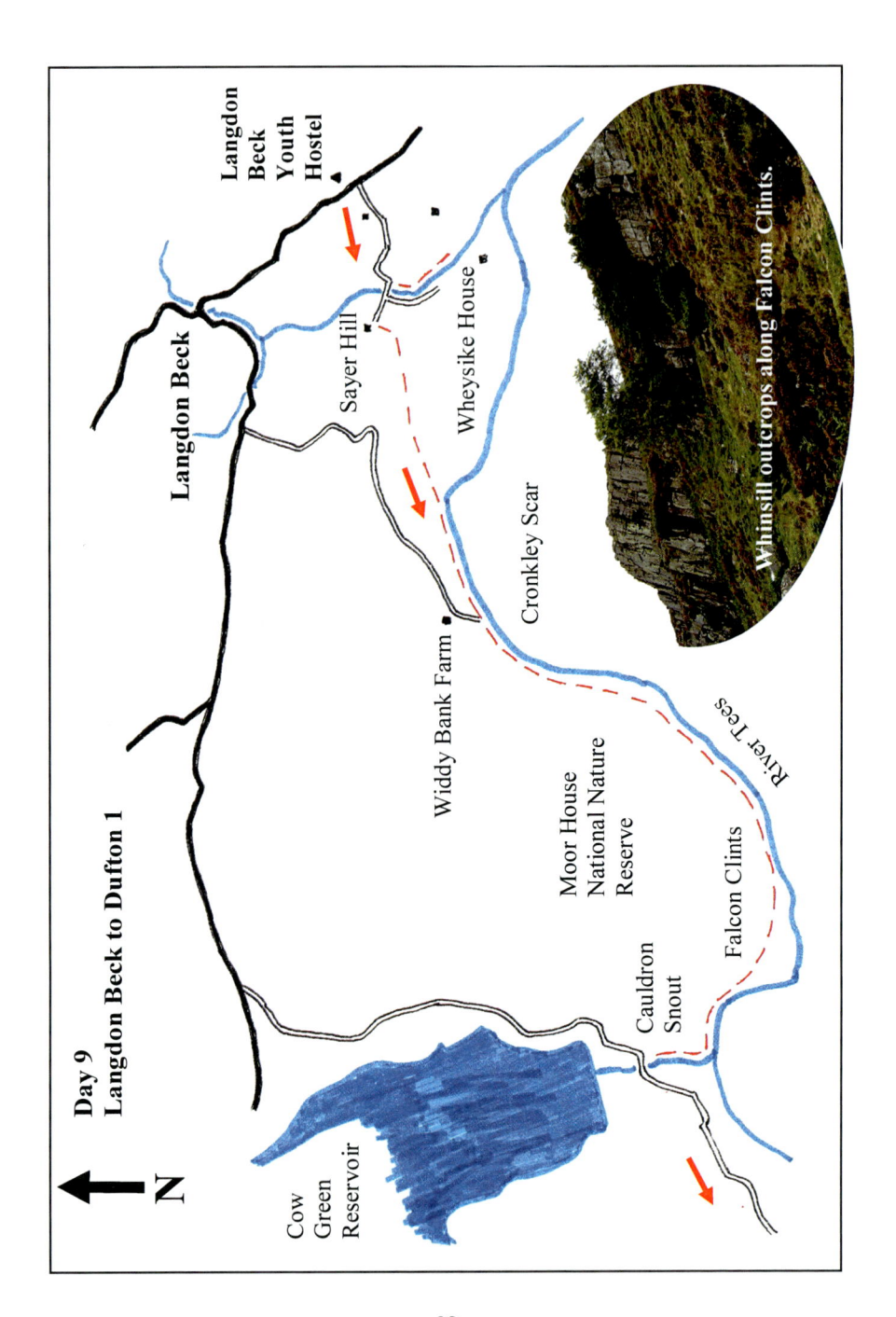

N

Langdon Beck

Langdon Beck Youth Hostel

Sayer Hill

Wheysike House

Cronkley Scar

Widdy Bank Farm

Moor House National Nature Reserve

River Tees

Falcon Clints

Cauldron Snout

Cow Green Reservoir

Whinsill outcrops along Falcon Clints.

Day 9
Langdon Beck to Dufton 2

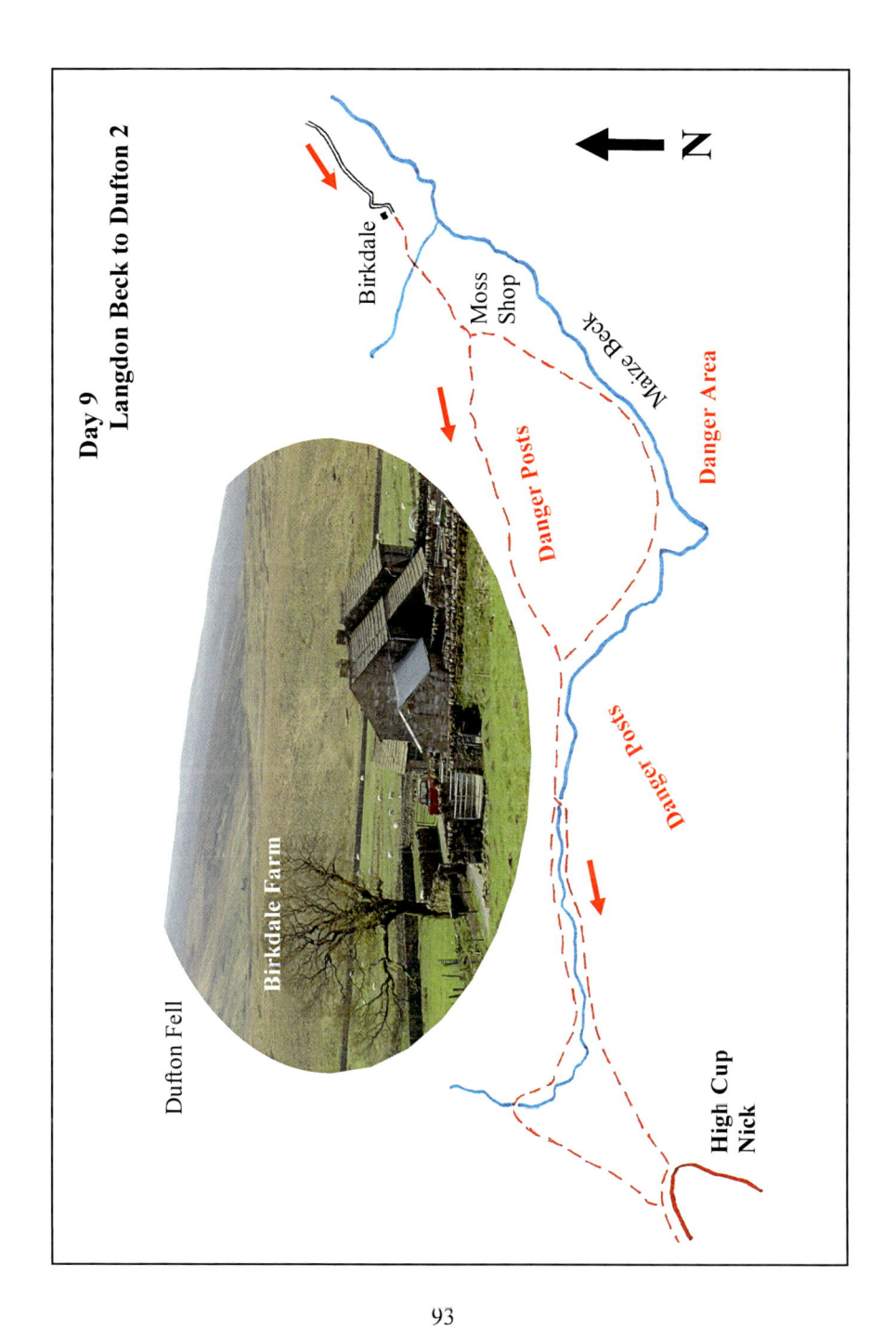

Birkdale

Moss Shop

Maize Beck

Danger Posts

Danger Area

Dufton Fell

Birkdale Farm

Danger Posts

High Cup Nick

N

Nichol Chair

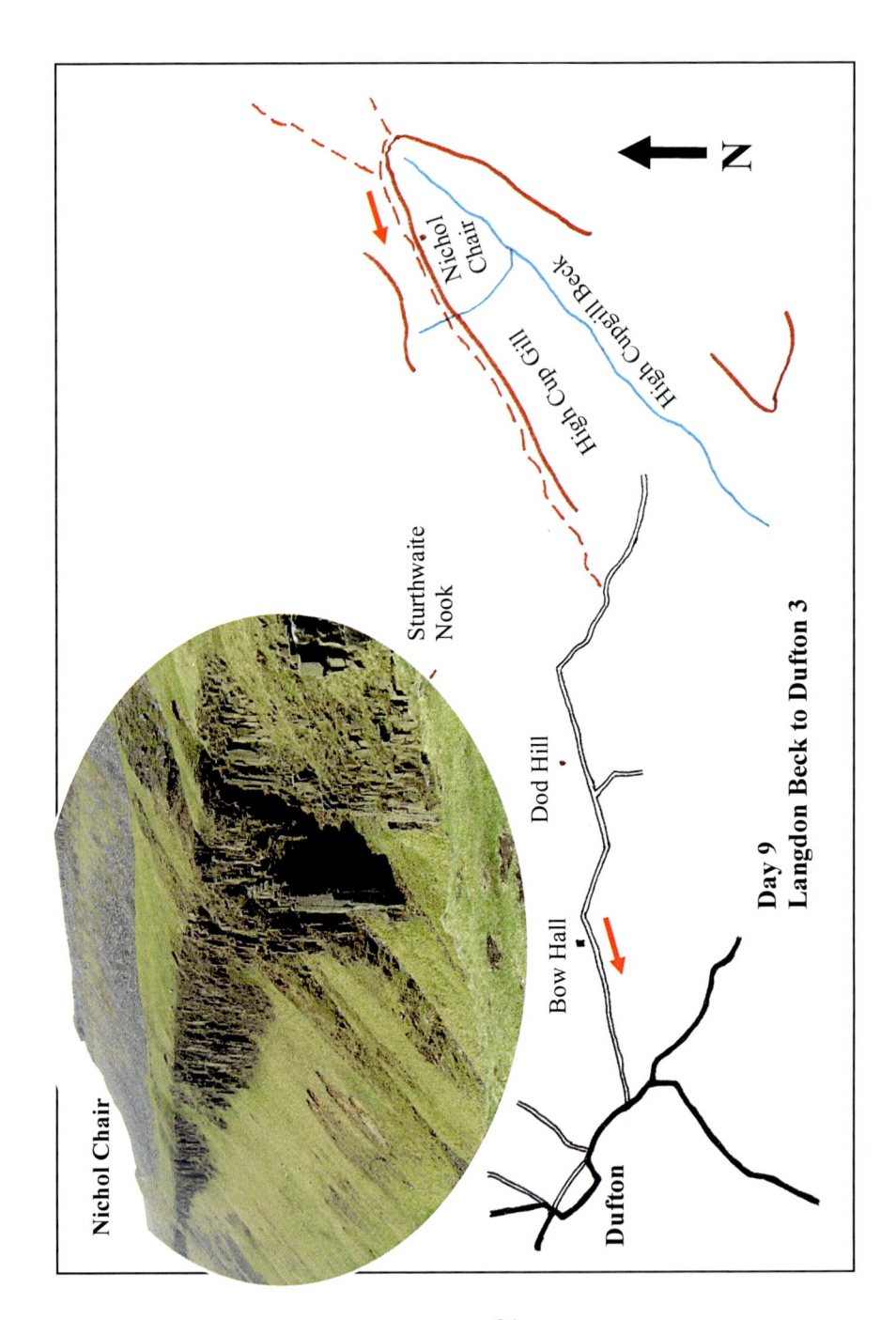

Sturthwaite Nook

Nichol Chair

High Cupgill Beck

High Cup Gill

Dod Hill

Bow Hall

Dufton

Day 9
Langdon Beck to Dufton 3

N

THE WALK

1. Turn back from the Youth Hostel and turn right down the track. Follow the track back to Saur Hill Bridge. Cross the bridge and carry straight on the track to Saur Hill Farm. The path continues and bears left in front of Widdybank Farm **[NY838 297]** alongside a fence to a stile. Bear right across a field to another stile. Enter Moor House National Nature Reserve and follow the clearly defined path, which eventually turns right to run alongside the north bank of the Tees.

Walking along the north bank of the Tees and, inset, a 'Welcome to Moor House' sign.

The path is well defined, but at times becomes a rocky scramble, before reaching the climb up alongside Cauldron Snout waterfall.

Not the highest waterfall, but one of the loudest and most dramatic, a torrent which drops 200' within 200 yards and an ideal place to sit and eat your packed lunch.

2. Cross the bridge **[NY814 287]** over the Tees just below Cow Green Reservoir. Follow the metalled track to Birkdale Farm, reputedly the highest inhabited farm in England. Pass through the farmyard and continue along the farm track. Pass through a large wooden gate and turn left over a footbridge over

Grain Beck [NY800 277]. Follow an artificial path up to Moss Shop.

This was the site of a crude bunkhouse, known as a shop, used by miners who only returned to their homes at the weekend.

3. Bear right on a path with the MoD firing range on the left hand side. The path eventually becomes a stone-flagged path running alongside a ditch and then a more indistinct route marked by posts, cairns and small clapper bridges before dropping down to Maize Beck [NY771 268].

Maize Beck on its way to join the River Tees and, inset, one of the marker stones alongside the path.

The path follows Maize Beck until you turn left over a footbridge and then right to follow the old miners' route to High Cup Nick.

A classic glacial U-shaped valley geological formation which is part of the well-known Whin Sill, and overlooks the best glaciated valley in Northern England. This is one of the most, if not the most, spectacular scenes on the whole of the walk – be careful if you suffer from vertigo!

4. Bear right to cross a stream [NY745 262] at the head of High Cup and then follow the path along the right hand side of the valley. The path eventually

High Cup.

drops down to a drove road which leads into Dufton. Turn right at Town Head past Brow Farm B&B and then in Dufton bear left and bear right into the main street. The Youth Hostel is on the left hand side. The Stag Inn is on the right **[NY989 251]**.

DAY 10: DUFTON TO GARRIGILL
Ancient clapper bridge over Great Rundale Beck

DAY 10: DUFTON TO GARRIGILL

I will start the introduction to today's walk with a serious warning. This is a very long section over some very high, desolate, featureless and unremitting fells with little shelter. Even in the summer the weather can deteriorate rapidly with hailstorms common. In poor conditions finding your way down from the highest point can be extremely difficult. Only attempt this if you are fit, well equipped and capable of using a compass. In poor weather it would be foolhardy for all but the most experienced fell walker to attempt this section. Oh, and just to make it sound even more tempting, Cross Fell (aka Fiend's Fell) is believed to be inhabited by evil spirits - look it up on Wikipedia!

Should you decide to give this section a miss, there is a good taxi company based in Appleby which I have used a couple of times – Morris Minor Travel, Tel 017683 52772 (www.morrisminortravel.co.uk). This would cost you £50, but I can only reiterate just how difficult and dangerous this section can be in poor conditions – the mountain rescue team is called out at least once a fortnight to Cross Fell.

Having said all that, it is still one of my favourite sections of the walk. There is a succession of ascents – Knock Fell, Great Dun Fell, Little Dun Fell and finally Cross Fell and the infamous meteorological phenomenon known as the Helm Wind. The walk is strenuous, it is a long day, but the views, if you get them, are incomparable. You are guaranteed a story to tell to fellow-walkers.

There are no refreshments available so a good packed lunch is essential. Thanks to Trudy of Coneygarth B&B for mine! Greg's Hut does, however, provide a very welcome shelter in which to rest and eat your lunch.

Today's destination is Garrigill, a delightful village which was badly affected by the closure of its local pub, the George and Dragon, a few years back (www.garrigillpub.co.uk). Thankfully now reopened with food served from 6-9 pm and a range of real ales. There are three B&B's but as the village is at the intersection of the Pennine Way and the Coast to Coast bike ride I would advise booking well in advance.
East View B&B (www.garrigillbedandbreakfast.co.uk) 01434 381561.
Bridge View B&B (www.bridgeview.org.uk) 01434 382448.
Garrigill Post Office Guest House (www.garrigill-guesthouse.co.uk) 01434 381257.
Should you fail to book accommodation you will have to continue a further three miles to Alston where details of accommodation can be found at www.visitcumbria.com/pen/alston.htm.

DISTANCE: 16 miles.
ASCENT: 3,490'
TERRAIN: Paths, muddy or boggy in places, and tracks.
TIME: 8 hours
START: Dufton
MAPS: OL31 North Pennines Teesdale and Weardale
OL19 Howgill Fells and Upper Eden Valley

FGS Grading
Grading F11 [D2, N2, T2, R3, H2]

Distance	2	12 – 18 miles
Navigation	2	Competent navigation skills needed
Terrain	2	25-50% on graded track or path, 50-75% off track
Remoteness	3	Remote, isolated location
Height gain	2	Over 125 ft per mile

Day 10
Dufton to Garrigill 1

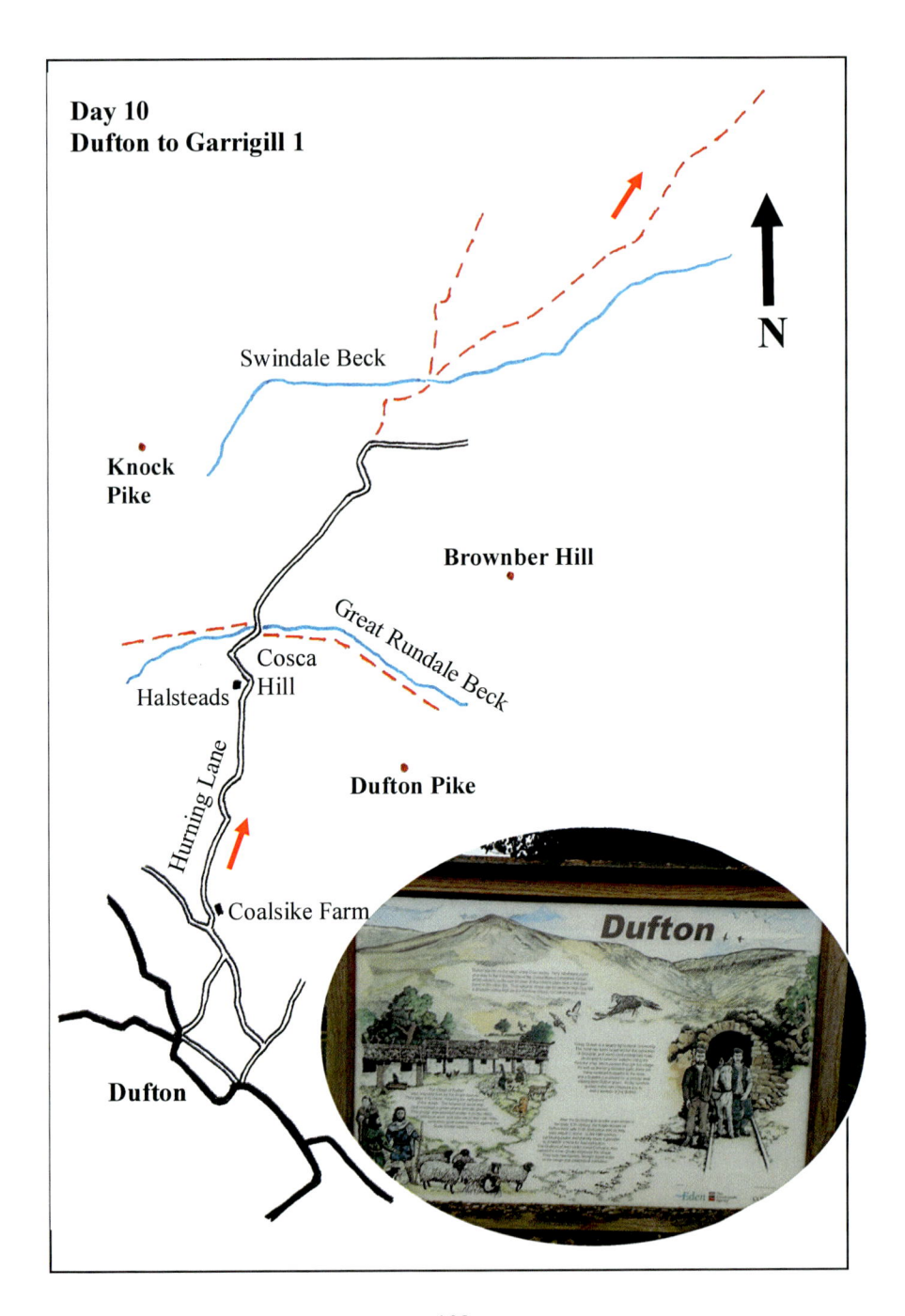

Swindale Beck

Knock Pike

Brownber Hill

Great Rundale Beck

Cosca Hill
Halsteads

Hurning Lane

Dufton Pike

Coalsike Farm

Dufton

**Day 10
Dufton to Garrigill 2**

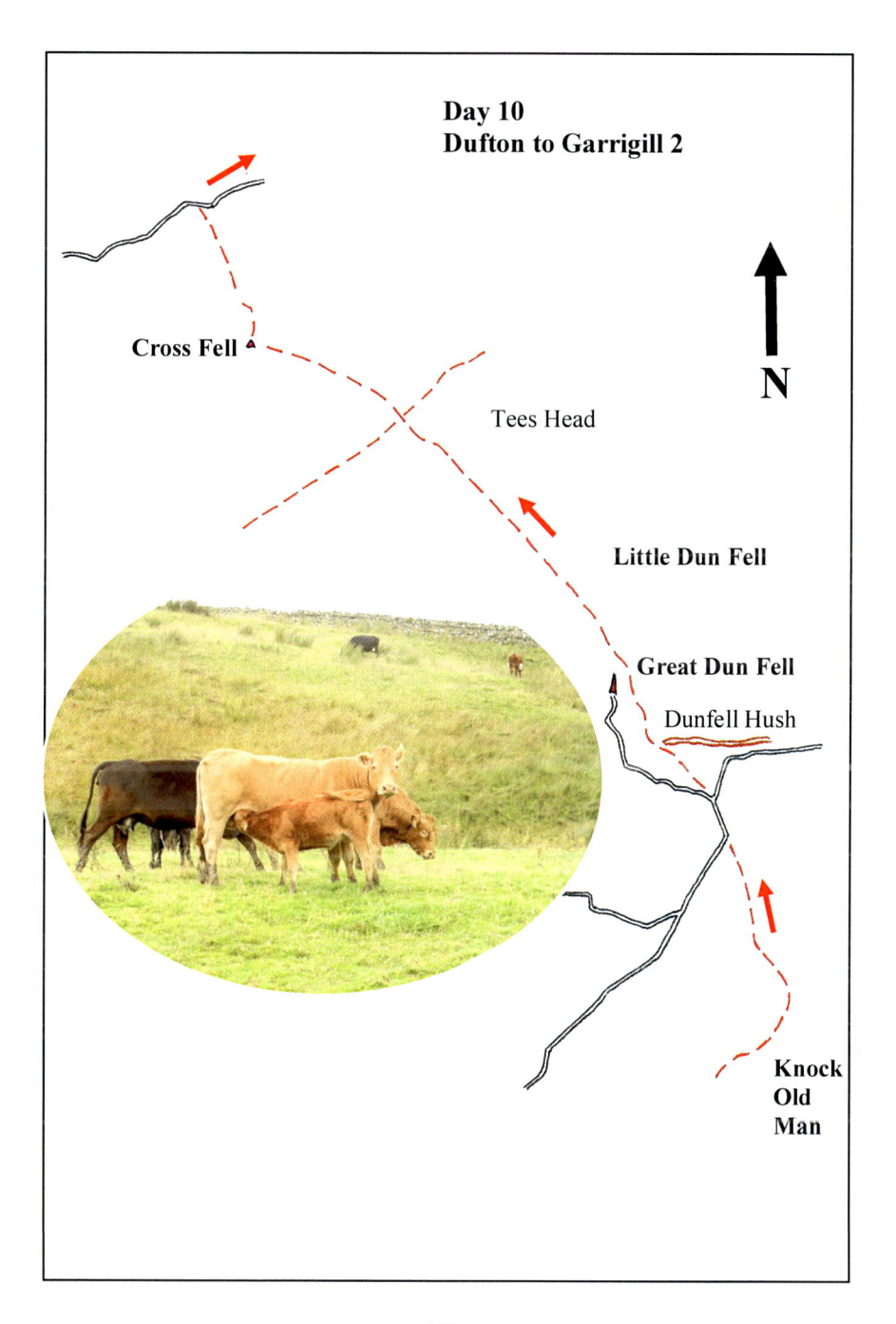

N

Cross Fell

Tees Head

Little Dun Fell

Great Dun Fell

Dunfell Hush

Knock
Old
Man

Garrigill

Black Band

Black Band

A

The George and Dragon, Garrigill.

Black Band

A

Pikeman Hill

Long Man Hill

Backstone Edge

Mine Workings

Mine Workings

Greg's Hut

Cross Fell

**Day 10
Dufton to Garrigill 3**

THE WALK

1. Turn left from the Youth Hostel (or right from the Stag Inn). The road bears right and then take the second footpath on the right up a hawthorn-lined track. Pass through Coatsike Farm **[NY689 259]** into Hurning Lane, an old miners' track. Continue northwards past Halsteads and contour around Cosca Hill before turning left to cross Great Rundale beck via an old clapper bridge **[NY692 273]**. Continue straight ahead, then shortly bear right up a walled track. The track eventually turns left over Small Burn and then bears right and north-eastwards.

2. Just before the top of the rise turn left along a path marked Pennine Way. Cross a stile and carry straight on to cross another stile. Take a footbridge over Swindale Beck **[NY700 285]**.

Bridge over the Swindale Beck.

Ignore a stile on the left hand side. The way heads steeply north-eastwards along a cairned path until it reaches the cairn of Knock Old Man **[NY720 301]** and then the summit of Knock Fell (2,604'). The way now changes direction and heads northwards past abandoned mine workings to reach a road **[NY717 314]**. At a bend in the road the Pennine Way leaves the road and heads upwards passing Dunfell Hush on your right and a radar station on your left. **[NY711 321]**.

There are many hushes in this area. Hushing is a method using a flood or torrent of water to reveal mineral veins – a temporary dam would be created and then the water suddenly released to, hopefully, reveal mineral deposits. The radar station is operated by the Civil Aviation Authority. There have been many reports of UFO activity in this area and 4 plane crashes, including 2 Tornadoes colliding, and a Halifax bomber in 1943.

The radar station on Great Dun Fell.

3. Continue over Great Dun Fell (2,780'). The path drops and then rises over Little Dun Fell (2,761') **[NY704 330]** and onwards on a stone-slabbed path to Cross Fell, at 2,930' the highest point in the Pennines **[NY687 343]**.

From the shelter head north-north-westwards following a line of cairns to turn right at a T-junction of tracks by a pile of stones **[NY684 352]**. The track continues to pass an emergency shelter, Greg's Hut.

Greg's Hut.

Greg's Hut was an old lead mining building. It was restored in 1972 by friends of John Gregory in his memory. John died in a tragic climbing accident in the Alps in 1968. It is maintained by the Greg's Hut Association (www.culgaith.org.uk/Ghut.html) in collaboration with the Mountain Bothy Association and is the highest bothy in England.

4. Continue past old mine workings and eventually skirt to the left of Long Man Hill and then Pikeman Hill. The track is very well defined, ignore any tracks off to the right.

This track is known as Corpse Road. Corpse roads were used for transporting corpses from remote communities to consecrated burial grounds. These routes developed in late medieval times and are also known by a number of other names: bier road, burial road, coffin road, coffin line, lyke or lych way, funeral road, procession way, corpse way.

5. The Pennine Way eventually bears right **[NY732 406]**, signposted Garrigill/ Pennine Way, and downhill, past a Methodist chapel into Garrigill **[NY745 415]**.

DAY 14: GARRIGILL TO HALTWHISTLE
The South Tyne Trail.

DAY 11: GARRIGILL TO HALTWHISTLE

From one of the more challenging day's walking to one of the easiest as we leave the Pennine Way. At Alston every guide book I have ever read acknowledges that the Pennine Way becomes less enjoyable. Today's walk instead follows the South Tyne Trail along a disused railway track. The Haltwhistle to Alston railway opened in 1852 and involved the construction of many bridges and nine viaducts. The railway finally closed in 1976.

As it is a shorter day there is time to explore Alston. There are many shops in Alston, as well as cash machines. At Alston Station you will find The Hub (**www.alston-hub.org.uk**). Open from 11am, this is a small museum of the history of Alston Moor with vintage vehicles, photographs and memorobilia. At Alston Station you will also find the narrow gauge South Tynedale Railway (**www.strps.org.uk**) – steam trains at 11am on certain days of the year if you want to let the train take the strain for just over 2 miles!

Refreshments between Alston and Haltwhistle can be obtained at the Wallace Arms, 4 miles from the end of the walk. Tel 01434 321872.

Haltwhistle claims to be the geographical centre of Britain and has its own, very neat, website at **www.haltwhistle.org**. Here you can find details of accommodation. As it is the penultimate stop on my last trip I treated myself to a stay at the Centre of Britain Hotel (**www.centre-of-britain.org.uk**), Tel 01434 322422 and was impressed. Haltwhistle is on the main Newcastle to Carlisle railway line and is a most agreeable little town.

DISTANCE:	18 miles.
ASCENT:	Negligible (the disused railway actually drops more than 500' in 13 miles).
TERRAIN:	Almost entirely on well-surfaced paths.
TIME:	6 hours
START:	Garrigill
MAPS:	OL31 North Pennines Teesdale and Weardale
	OL43 Hadrian's Wall Haltwhistle and Hexham

FGS Grading
Grading T3 [D2, N0, T0, R1, H0]

Distance	2	12-18 miles
Navigation	0	No navigation skills needed
Terrain	0	75%+ on graded track or path
Remoteness	1	Countryside in fairly close approximation to habitation
Height gain	0	Less than 100 ft per mile

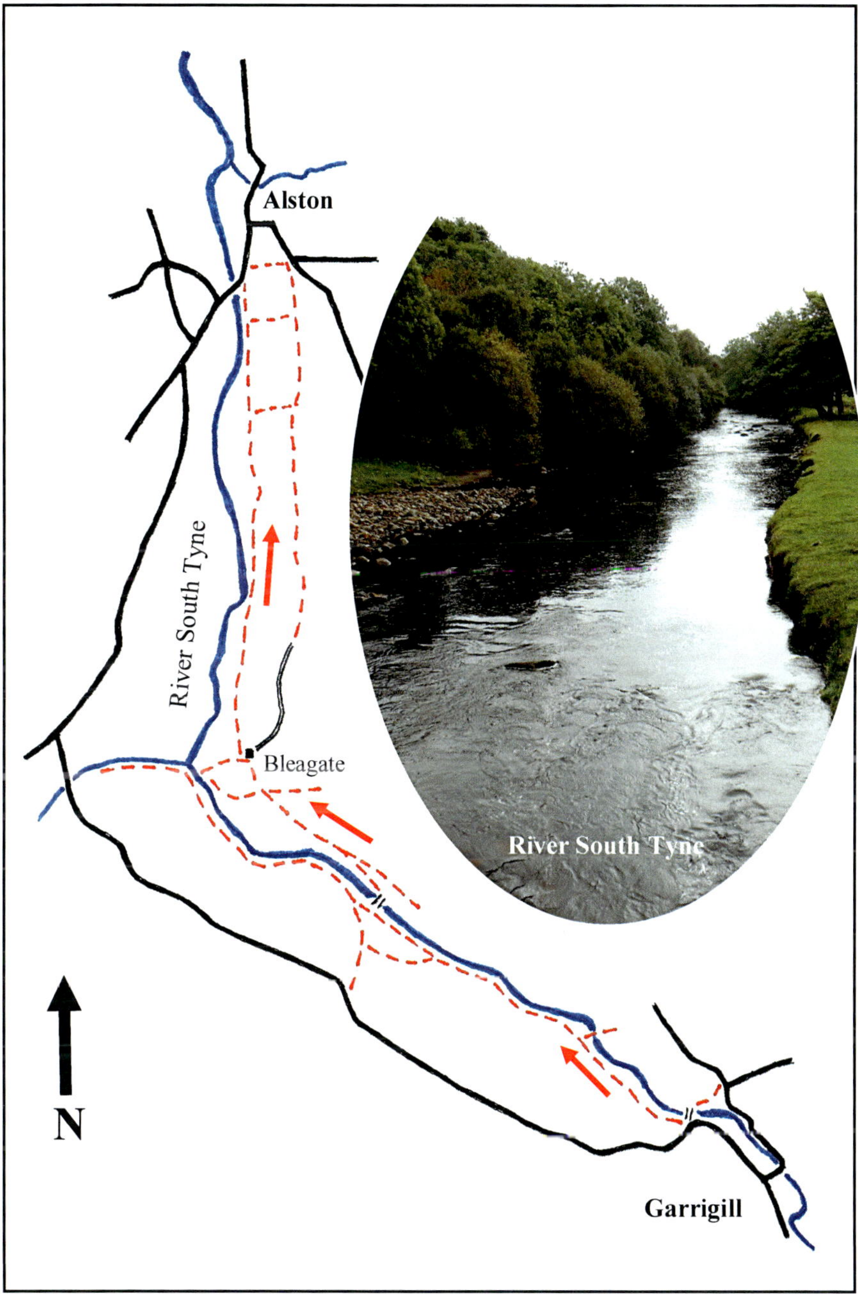
Alston
River South Tyne
Bleagate
River South Tyne
N
Garrigill

Slaggyford

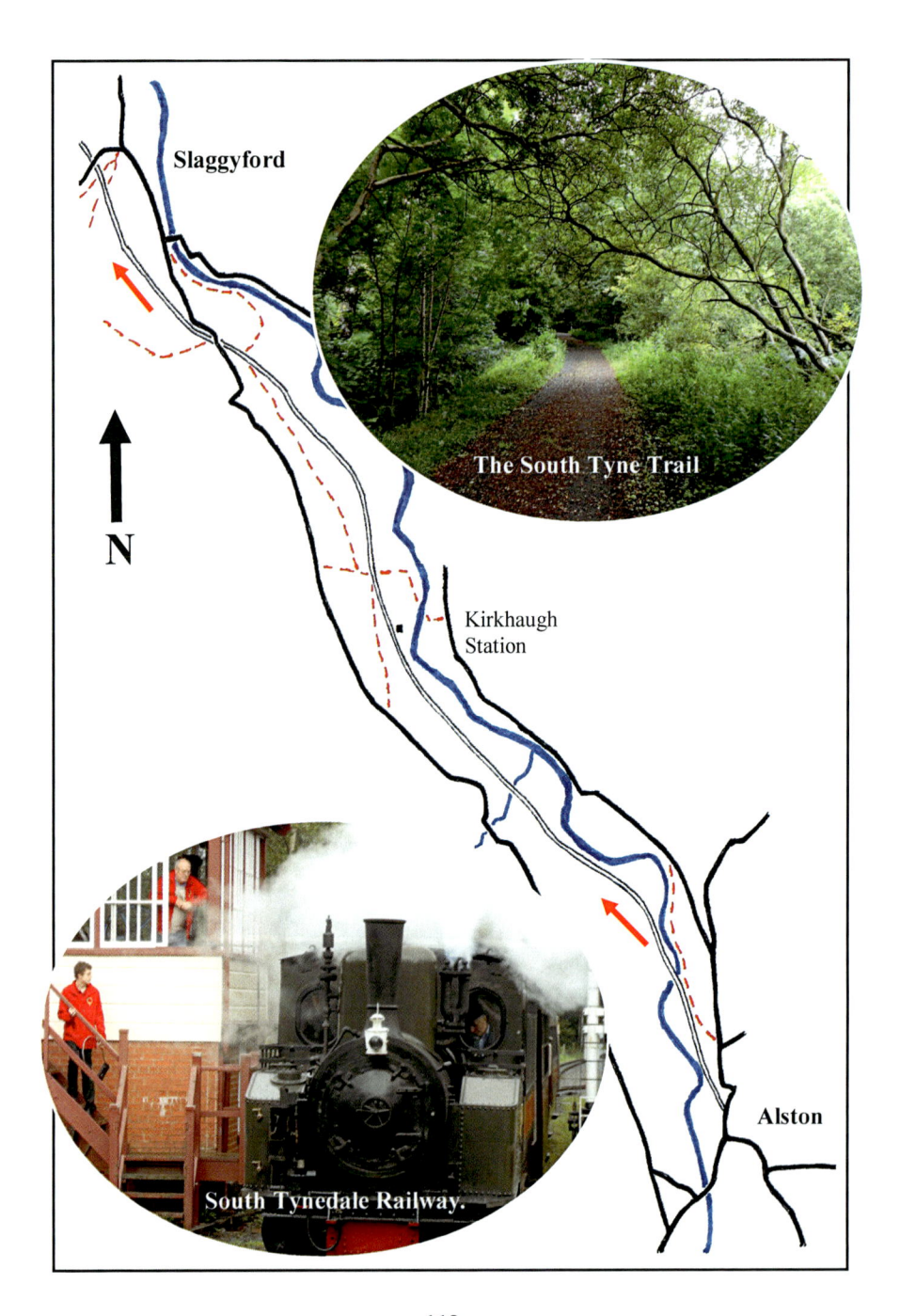

The South Tyne Trail

Kirkhaugh
Station

South Tynedale Railway.

Alston

Coanwood

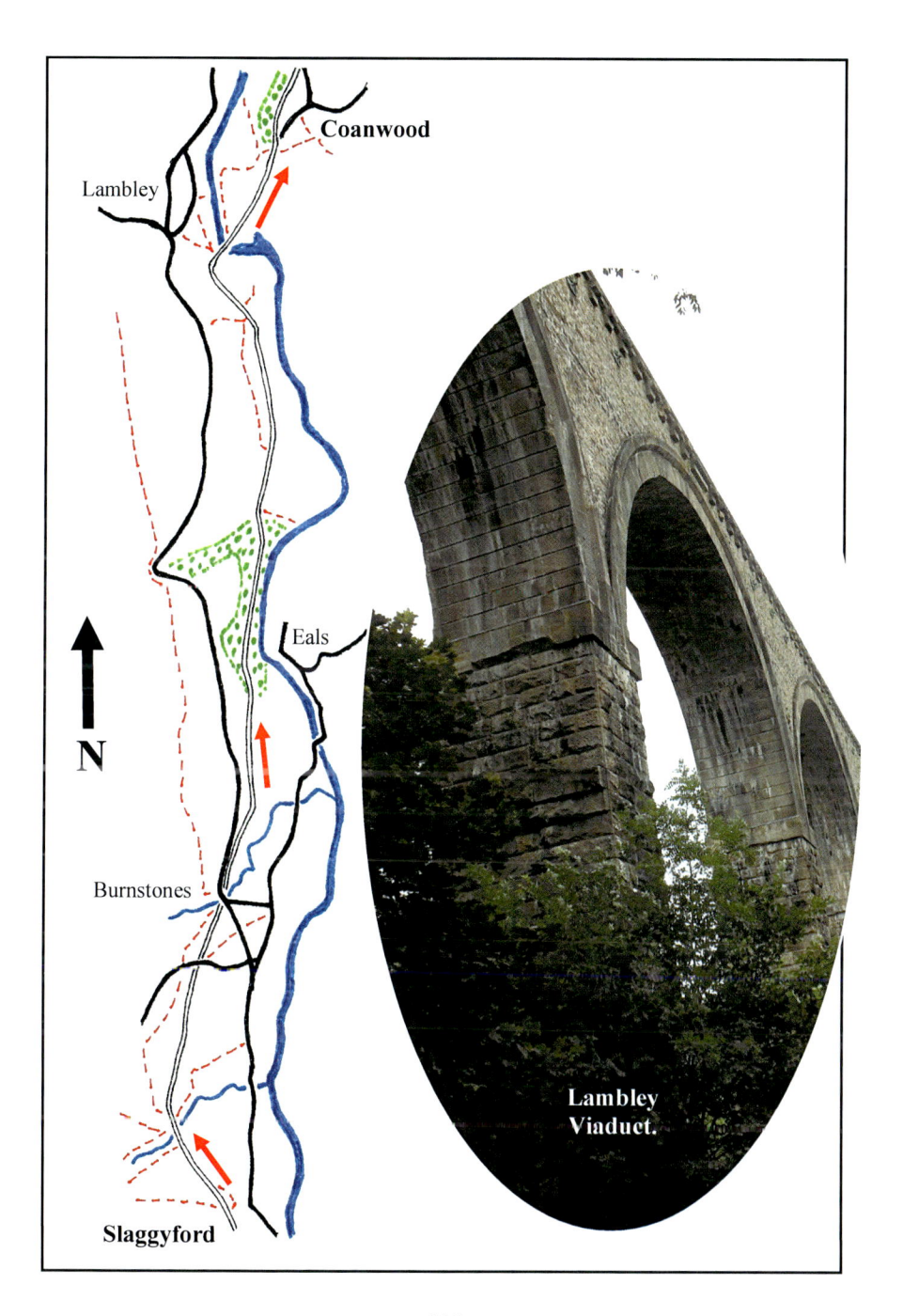

Lambley

Eals

N

Burnstones

Slaggyford

Lambley Viaduct.

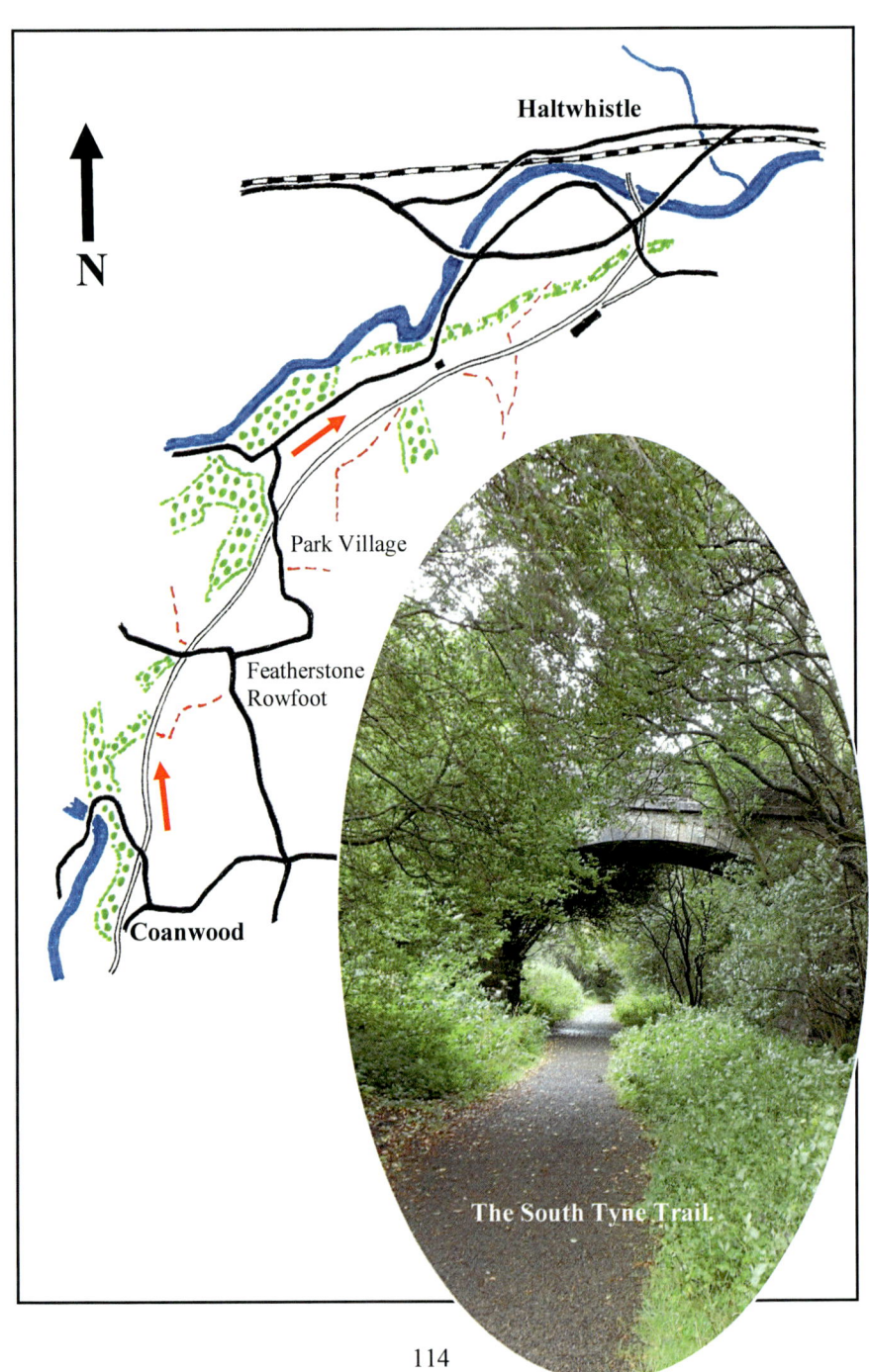

Haltwhistle

Park Village

Featherstone
Rowfoot

Coanwood

The South Tyne Trail.

THE WALK

1. Head north-westwards up the main street out of Garrigill, where the road bears uphill cross a stile on your right **[NY740 418]** to eventually join a riverside path. The path crosses a footbridge onto the opposite bank **[NY724 429]**. When the path bears right uphill follow a stone wall for a short distance before bearing right and continuing uphill. Continue to follow the clearly signposted path to Alston. At the end of the path (just after passing the Youth Hostel), turn left onto a minor road and almost immediately turn right onto the A686.

The River South Tyne.

2. Walk northwards up the A686 (Station Road) to Alston Station at the north end of the town **[NY717 467]**. Cross the level crossing and follow the path which runs alongside the narrow-gauge steam railway as far as Lintley Railway Station. South Tynedale Railway (www.south-tynedale-railway.org.uk).

Just over a mile out of Alston you can see the medieval peel tower of Randalhome Farm. At Gildersdale Viaduct you may be lucky enough to see the red squirrels. Soon after the viaduct you can see the grassy ramparts of the Roman fort of Whitley Castle which was situated on the Roman road of Maiden Way. This ran between Kirkby Thore, near Appleby and Carvoran Fort on

Hadrian's Wall. This was the heart of the territory of the native Bringanteum and so the road would be part of the roman efforts to control them.

3. The trail continues along the disused railway track through the disused railway station of Slaggyford (The ultimate destination for the narrow gauge railway line).

The trail passes through Whitwam Farm which is in the Countryside Stewardship Scheme. This was established to encourage farmers to operate in ways which support the environment. As a direct result of this initiative curlews, lapwings and redshanks have had their habitat protected on this farm.

4. The route continues on to Lambley Station. Here you have to take a stepped path down to the right, walk under the viaduct and then climb back to the track via steps and a steel staircase. Cross Lambley Viaduct and peer over the edge if you dare!

Lambley Viaduct.

In 1991 the British Rail Property Board repaired the viaduct and handed it to the North Pennine Heritage. It is an elegant example of Victorian engineering with nine arches and is 105' high.

5. Next station is Coanwood and then Featherstone Park station. Turn right here for the Wallace Arms which is open every lunchtime. The track continues through Park Village until the disused railway line ends at Plenmeller

Track bed of former railway.

Road. Turn left towards the bypass and take the path to the right of the minor road opposite to the right. Turn right onto the path which takes you upwards and then curves back onto the impressive Alston Arches viaduct **[NY709 636]**. This crosses the South Tyne and leads you directly on to Haltwhistle Station. Cross the railway footbridge to gain access to the town centre **[NY706 640]**.

DAY 12: HALTWHISTLE TO WALTON
A section of the restored Hadrian's Wall just after Walltown Crags.

DAY 12: HALTWHISTLE TO WALTON

Today's walk largely follows the Hadrian's Wall National Trail through some beautiful scenery. Building the wall through such terrain, and in weather which can at times be quite inhospitable was an incredible achievement. The wall was built in less than six years. There are some stunning views to be had on today's walk.

Refreshments are available at Walltown Quarry, Carvoran Roman Army Museum and Birdoswald Roman Fort (you have to pay to enter the museum in the fort in order to access the cafes – Carvoran's hot food was excellent last time I stopped and the museum is well worth a visit). At Gisland, just over 8 miles into the walk, you will find the excellent House of Meg tearooms. An hour from the end of the walk is Haytongate Hut, self-service, where you can make yourself a brew and put money in the honesty box.

This is quite a long day's walk. Apart from the scenery it also includes the Roman Museums at Carvoran and Birdoswald, Thirlwall Castle and Lanercost Priory. To do justice to these you may wish to split today into two separate days by taking a break just after Gisland at Willowford Farm (**www.willowford.co.uk**), Tel 016977 47962. Willowford Farm has a wide range of rooms available and a superb website.

If you are completing this in one day there is a variety of accommodation available near to Walton. The Centurion Inn is now closed (and in view of my experience of its food and hospitality, that is not surprising). My last stay was at Sandysike Farm, Tel 016977 2330, which is shortly after Walton, directly on (and partially constructed from!) Hadrian's Wall – a much more pleasant experience. A mile north of Walton is Walton High Rigg Farm (**www.waltonhighrigg.co.uk**), Tel 016977 2117. Also just north of Walton is Low Rigg Farm (**www.lowriggfarm.co.uk**), Tel 016977 3233. This is another B&B which I can personally recommend and is only ten minutes walk from Walton.

DISTANCE:	17.5 miles
ASCENT:	950'
TERRAIN:	Paths and tracks
TIME:	8.5 hours
START:	Haltwhistle
MAPS:	OL43 Hadrian's Wall, Haltwhistle and Hexham
	315 Carlisle

FGS Grading
Grading T6 [D3, N1, T1, R1, H0]

Distance	3	18 miles +
Navigation	1	Basic navigation skills needed
Terrain	1	50 - 75% on graded track or path
Remoteness	1	Countryside in fairly close proximity to habitation
Height gain	0	Less than 100 ft per mile

Aesica Roman Fort

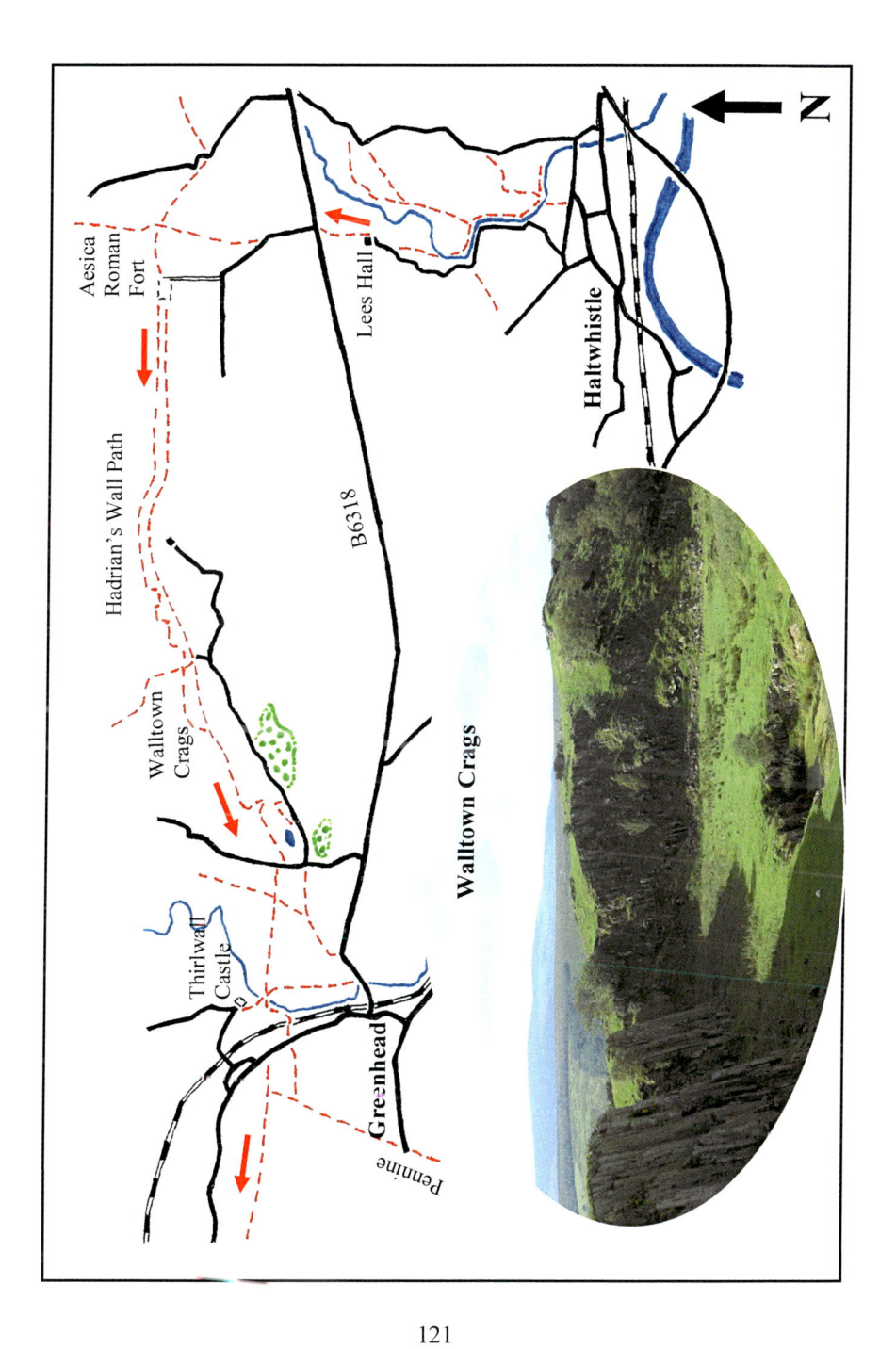

Lees Hall

Haltwhistle

Hadrian's Wall Path

B6318

Walltown Crags

Walltown Crags

Thirlwall Castle

Greenhead

Pennine

N

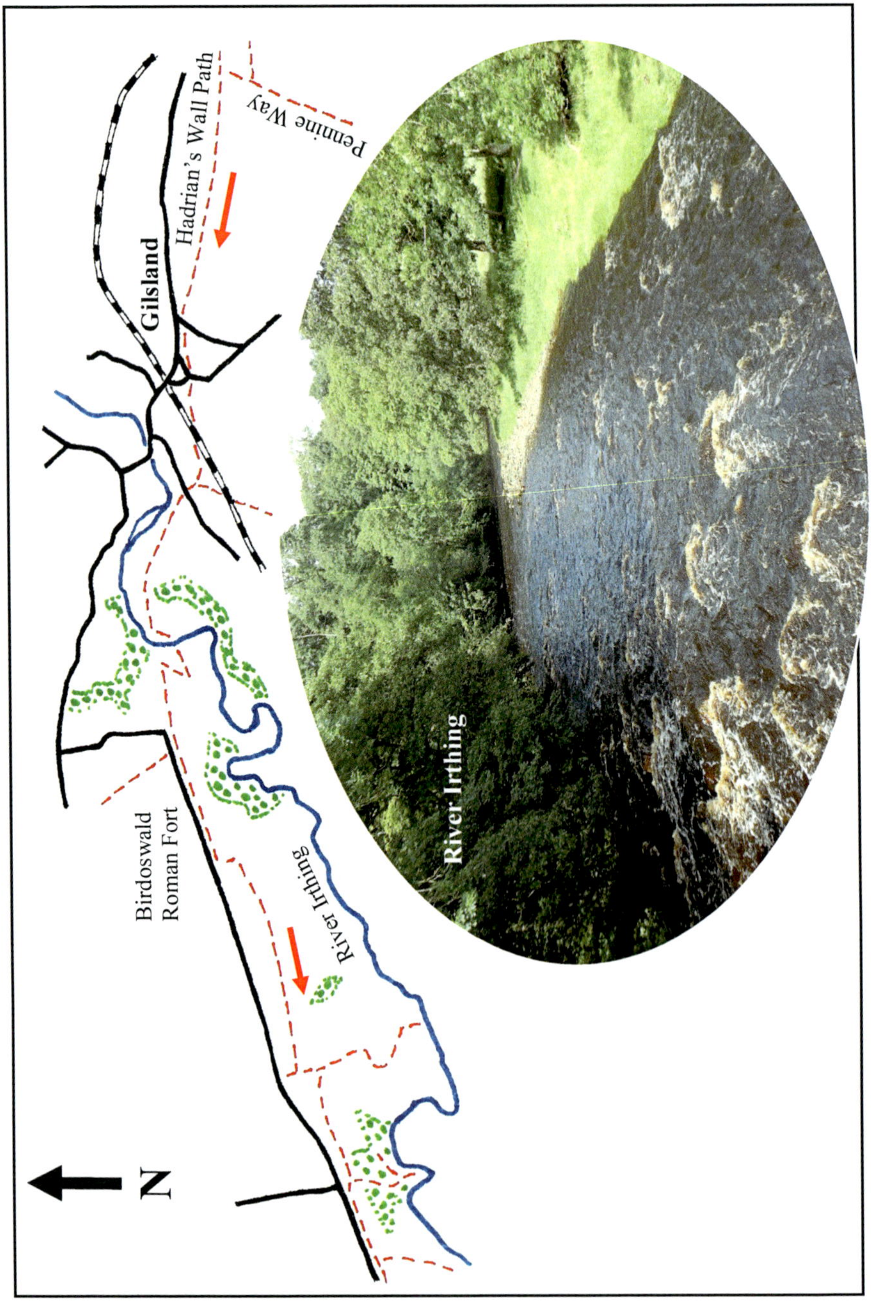
Gilsland
Hadrian's Wall Path
Pennine Way
Birdoswald
Roman Fort
River Irthing
River Irthing
N

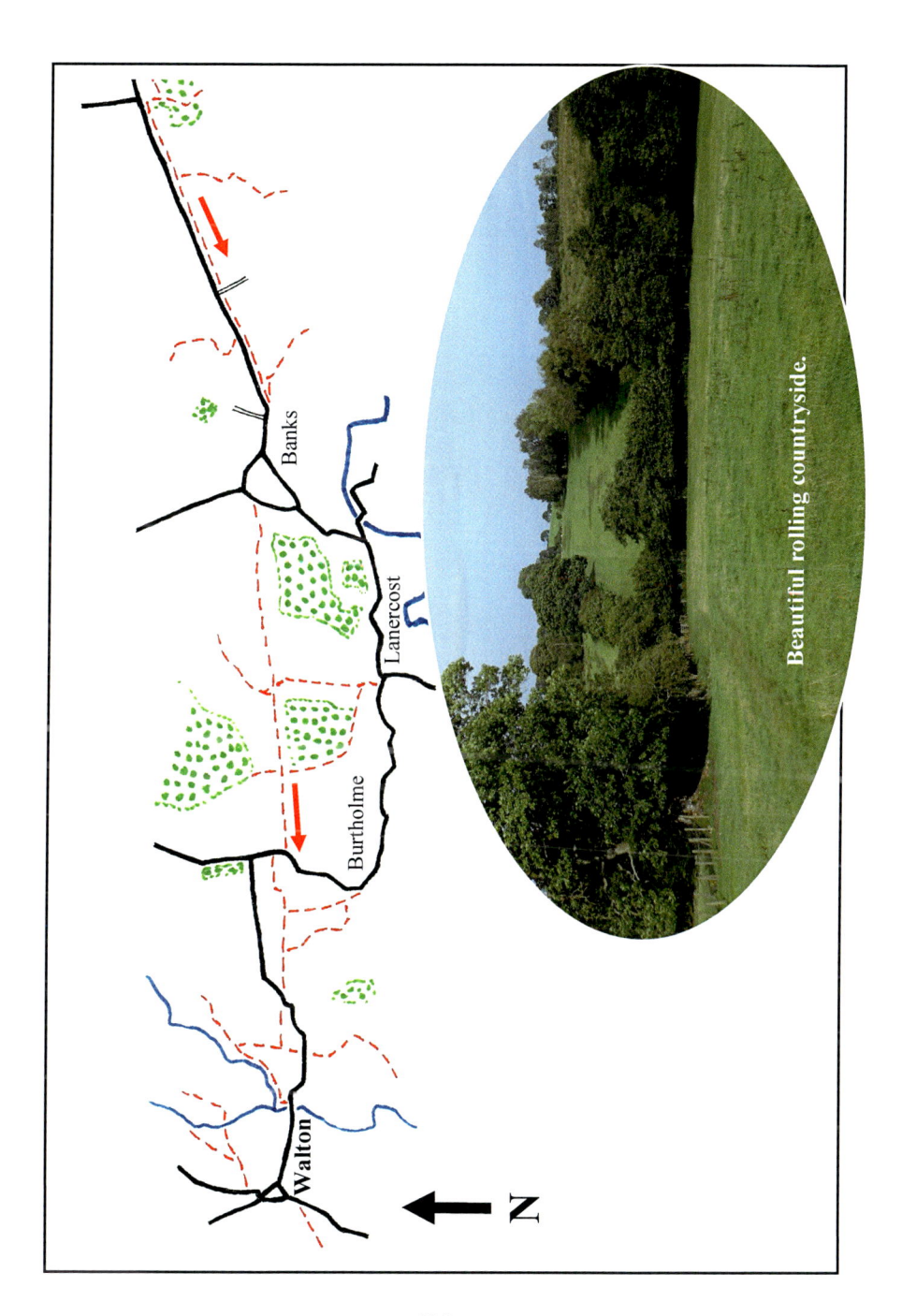

Beautiful rolling countryside.

THE WALK

1. Follow Westgate (the main street running away from the railway) into Main Street. Pass the Manor House Hotel on your right hand side and turn left up St James Lane. Pass through a supermarket car park and turn right onto a road. At the crest of the hill turn left up a private road. Carry straight on to a footpath which leads you to a footbridge over Haltwhistle Burn **[NY710 644]**. Cross the footbridge and turn left to follow the path alongside the burn. Keep to the better defined path which rises slightly above the burn. Continue along, ignoring a private bridge crossing the burn, to the Old Brickworks. Continue until you cross to the other side of the burn via a footbridge.

The burn and the gorge it runs through had several brickworks, two woollen mills, a coal mine, tile works and lime kilns. A wagonway ran through the gorge from Cawfields Quarry on Hadrian's Wall down to join the main Newcastle to Carlisle railway.

Haltwhistle Burn.

2. At this point turn left for a short distance back to a road. Turn right onto the road **[NY705 650]** which leads to Lees Hall. The track bears right and then left around Lees Hall and then continues northwards through a field to a main road **[NY707 658]**. There was a bull in this field, the farmer told me that it was a friendly bull from Gloucestershire(!) but kindly offered to walk through the field with me. Turn right onto the main road and then immediately left onto a lane. The lane bears left and you then take a path on the right hand side **[NY707 662]**. Follow the wall, which is on your right hand side, then cross a ladder stile to continue to follow it on the other side. This path takes you over the course of the Roman vallum and then to the Hadrian's Wall national trail **[NY707 668]**. Turn left over a stile and follow the path. You will shortly reach the site of Aesica or Great Chesters fort.

Little is left of the actual fort, but its outline can clearly be seen. If you look to the eastern side of the south gate you can discern a carving of a jug on a squat stone pillar. This was an altar.

3. Continue with the Roman wall to your right. Cross 2 stiles to pass a stone house near the trees. Enter the woods and turn right to follow the path which runs between mixed and conifer woodlands. Upon leaving the woodland the path continues along the spine of a hill and rises up on a crag. Keep the farm wall on your right hand side.

4. The path rises over a succession of spectacular crags until you reach Turret 44B. At Turret 44B the wall and path turn left at a right angle. Follow a flagged path carefully downhill. When the flagged path ends continue in the same direction straight over a farm track **[NY680 666]**. The path climbs uphill and bears right. Bear right again and follow the top of Walltown Crags (in poor weather, a more defined, lower level path can be followed). Follow the top of the crag carefully as there is a sheer drop which is unfenced in places. You will follow a well-preserved section of Roman wall including Turret 45A, an excellent place to pause for a breather.

This section of the wall is authentic and has not been subjected to 19th Century reconstruction. John Clayton was a 19th Century lawyer, who saw local farmers helping themselves to the stones of the wall. He began purchasing the land to prevent this happening. Eventually he owned large areas of land including the sites of Chesters, Carrawburgh, Housesteads and Vindolanda. He also funded the careful reconstruction of several sections of wall. Turret 45A was built before Hadrian's Wall as a lookout tower and was later incorporated into the wall as it was built.

5. Continue along the path until it ends abruptly at a field wall. Follow the field wall downhill and then turn right through a wooden kissing gate into Walltown

Restored wall near Willowford.

Vague traces of Hadrian's Wall.

Quarry. Turn right onto the gravel path around the north side of the lake. At this point refreshments can be obtained from a small National Trust cafe.

Refreshments and seating are limited here - continue and turn left a short distance up the road to reach the Roman Army Museum on the site of the Roman fort known as Magna (rock) or Carvoran (www.vindolanda.com). A very well presented museum, open 10am to 6pm, with an excellent cafe and hot food. The museum shows video of a birds-eye view of the entire wall and a computer generated reconstruction of how the wall would originally have looked.

6. Carry on and turn right onto a road. [Turn back and straight on if you have been to Carvoran.] Just before a cattle grid turn left **[NY668 660]**. The walk continues across 2 fields with the ditch to your left. At the end of the 2nd field follow a path down to cross a footbridge. The path climbs to pass the ruins of Thirlwall Castle.

Thirlwall Castle was heavily fortified to protect the owners from cross-border raiders (reivers). Thirlwall is derived from the local dialect for 'Gap in the Wall' and it was built in the 14th Century from stones taken from the wall.

Thirlwall Castle.

7. Opposite the entrance to the ruins turn left on to the field path by the stream. Carry straight on to cross the stream again and go over the railway to reach a road. Turn right onto the road and go past the entrance to the golf club. Take some steps up the bank on the left hand side to a stile **[NY656 660]**. Continue straight ahead with the field wall on your right and passing a farm on the left hand side. Cross a stile and a footbridge and the path runs along the southern side of the ditch. After the next footbridge the path goes around the farm buildings to reach a farm track. Turn right onto the farm track to the next stile on the left hand side. Continue in a straight line across the fields. On reaching the road turn right and then immediately left onto the footpath running alongside the road. The path follows the line of the ditch until it meets a road.

8. Cross straight over the road and cross a field to pass through a small wooden gate. Drop down right towards the railway. Do not go under the railway, but carry straight on alongside the railway on a well made path. Continue along this path, over a footbridge and up some steps. Pass Milecastle 48 **[NY634 662]** and continue on the path to cross the railway. Follow the grassy path over a stone clapper bridge and then along a flagged path to the road.

Milecastle 48, also known as Poltross Burn Milecastle, is in excellent condition. Many signs around the site tell you about its history and the clues about the history of the wall which it has revealed to archaeologists.

9. Turn right onto the road (continue straight on for five minutes for the House of Meg tearooms) and then immediately left. The walk continues on a path to the right alongside a section of exposed wall and the outline of Turret 48A. Follow the path around the back of Willowford Farm.

This is a good place to stay if you are breaking this chapter into two separate day's walking.

10. Continue with the wall on your left. Pass the remains of the Roman bridge of Willowford. Cross a large footbridge over the river Irthwell and follow a stone-flagged path which climbs up the hill and turn right onto a stone track which continues to climb. Turn left to follow the path on the left hand side of the wall. You reach a tree-lined path and then continue straight ahead on a road to the Roman fort of Birdoswald. You can also obtain coffee here.

Birdoswald once held over a thousand Roman soldiers. It contains the remains of a paved granary, a well preserved Roman gate and an excellent mu-

Willowford Bridge.

seum which gives details of the Roman occupation of the site and the history of this location.

11. Continue along the road for a short distance, then turn left through a kissing gate. Follow a path through a restored Victorian orchard and then double back to continue along the left hand side of the wall. Over the wall the road runs on top of the foundations of Hadrian's Wall. Cross a stile and then at the next field boundary turn left **[NY609 661]** and follow the field wall. At the top of the rise turn right over a stile and the path follows the fence alongside the earthworks of the original turf wall.

The Roman ditch lies immediately to your left, beyond that are the remains of the turf wall and beyond that the vallum. This is the only clearly visible remains of the original turf wall on the entire trail.

12. Cross straight over a farm track and then left onto the next farm track which runs alongside a wooded stream. Turn right to cross a bridge over Wall Burn and continue towards the trees with the Vallum on your right. Follow the fence to pass through a gate into the woods. Continue in the same direction through the woods and then turn right to return to the road. Turn left and continue past a single-storey house, where a stile takes you onto a path alongside the road. Continue through 2 stiles to a line of trees. Another stile in the corner of the field takes you back onto the road to pass farm buildings. A further stile after the buildings allows you to access the field path again. A gate in the corner of the field gives access to Pike Hill signal tower.

Pike Hill signal station is the only signal station on the wall. It was built by Agricola before the wall. The wall has an obvious kink in it so as to incorporate the signal station.

13. After the signal tower you cross a stile to resume the field path alongside the road. Rejoin the road to walk through the hamlet of Banks. Bear right where the road divides **[NY568 646]** and then left at the T-Junction. Turn next right towards Hare Hill. The road climbs up, passing a remnant of Roman wall. When the road bears right, carry straight on through a kissing gate. Keep to the edge of the field and pass through a gate to continue along a farm track. Pass over a drive to a farmhouse **[NY554 645]**.

Here you will find the famous Haytongate Hut (www.itrod.co.uk) – a small wooden summerhouse equipped with a fridge, kettle, coffee, milk and snacks. Help yourself, place your money in the honesty box and read the messages left by other walkers. If you are completing this section over 2 days you may at this point want to make a detour to Lanercost Priory (www.lanercostpriory.org.uk). The priory was built with stones taken from Hadrian's Wall in 1169. Well worth a visit, just turn left and walk approximately half a mile.

14. Continue on the path which drops downwards with splendid views of rolling hills, trees, fields and the Lake District Peaks in the distance. Cross over a footbridge and straight on up the field. Cross straight over a road, through a kissing gate and straight across the field to another kissing gate. Cross a farm track and carry straight on through the fields. At a minor road continue in the same direction past Hollybush Cottage. Turn right to follow the stream and then left along the riverbank. Join a road and at a junction turn right to walk into Walton **[NY522 643]**. Turn right for Low Rigg and High Rigg Farms. If you are staying at Sandysike Farm follow the first instructions of the next chapter.

DAY 13: WALTON TO CARLISLE
The River Eden.

DAY 13: WALTON TO CARLISLE

A short, but extremely pleasant walk through farm fields, woods and alongside the River Eden into Carlisle. I have walked this section in spring, summer and late autumn and always thoroughly enjoyed it. There is little to be seen of the wall now apart from traces of the earthworks, but today's destination has plenty to offer those who have an interest in history.

Refreshments are hardly needed on such a short walk, but there are two self-service points; basic refreshments at the Stall in the Wall, and a chance to make yourself a brew at High Crosby Farm. There is a pub, The Stag Inn, in Crosby-on-Eden, but unless you have made a late start, and are taking things very slowly, this is unlikely to be open by the time you get there.

DISTANCE: 12 miles
ASCENT: Negligible
TERRAIN: Paths and tracks
TIME: 4 hours
START: Walton
MAPS: 315 Carlisle

FGS Grading
Grading T3 [D1, N0, T1, R1, H0]

Distance	1	6-12 miles
Navigation	0	No navigation skills needed
Terrain	1	50 - 75% on graded track or path
Remoteness	1	Countryside in fairly close proximity to habitation
Height gain	0	Less than 100 ft per mile

Vague traces of the Wall still follow the path.

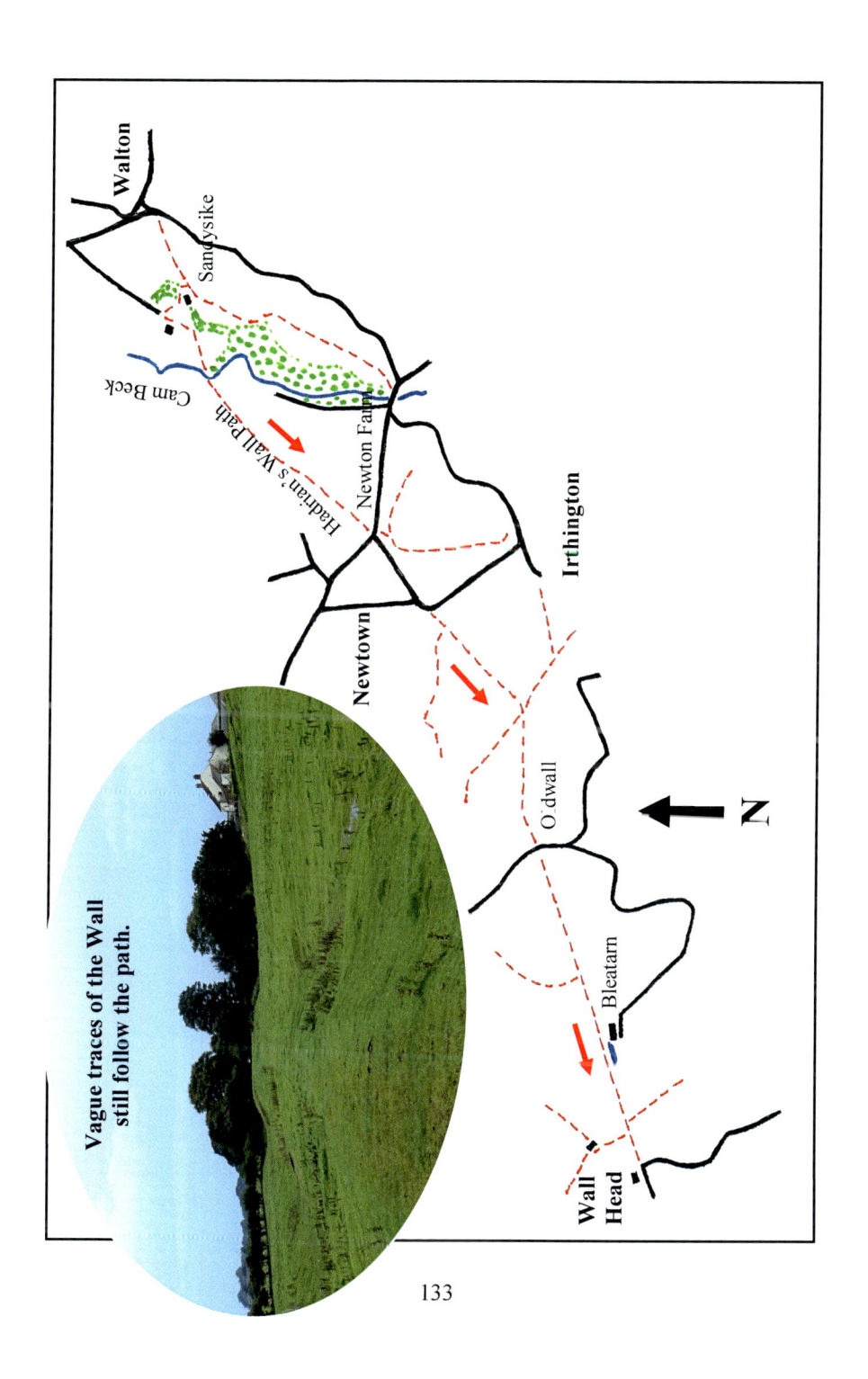

N

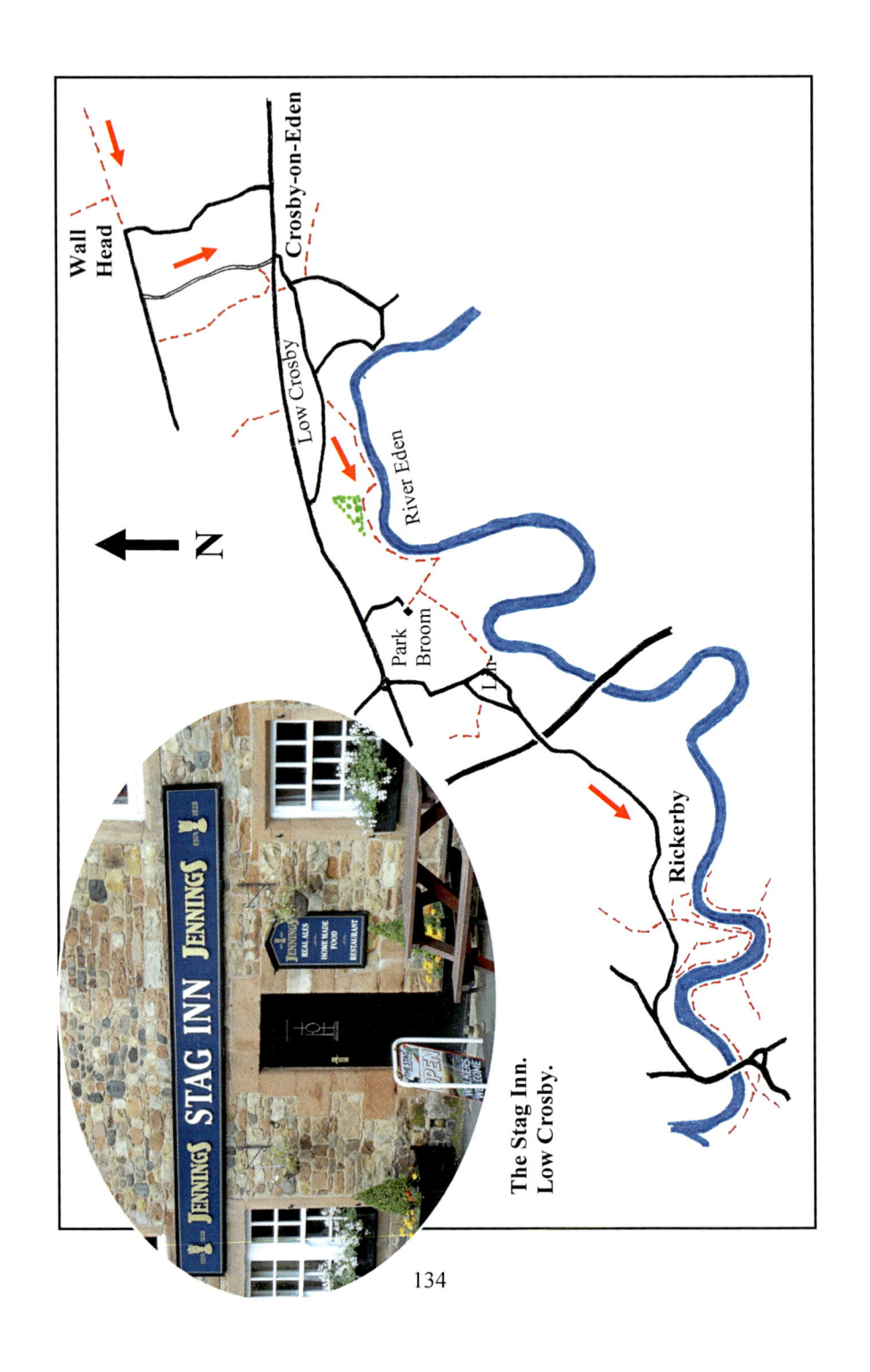

The Stag Inn.
Low Crosby.

The Memorial Bridge over the River Eden.

Rickerby

Carlisle Station

N

THE WALK

1. Continue westwards along the road out of Walton. Where the road bears left, turn right onto a track **[NY521 643]**. Follow the track with the hedge on your left hand side. Here the route goes through a kissing gate to the right of Sandysike Farm. [If you are staying at Sandysike carry straight on to the left of the farm buildings to reach the front of Sandysike Farm.]

Go through the kissing gate which takes you round the back of Sandysike Farm and into the wood. Cross a stone slab bridge and follow the obvious path through the trees. At the end of the wood turn right onto the farm road and then left to pass in front of a farm.

After passing the farm you reach a large wooden gate and then pass through a kissing gate opposite **[NY514 640]**. The line of the wall is now on your left. At the end of the field take the stone-flagged path down to a copse and the footbridge over Cam Beck. Cross the footbridge and turn left to follow the fence towards farm buildings. Follow signs around the farmyard and continue across the next field with the hedge on your left. Continue across the fields to reach some sandstone steps. Climb the sandstone steps to pass a sandstone house. Pass through a gate in the top right corner of the field and continue along the left hand side of a hedge. Join a lane which takes you towards Newtown Farm.

2. Cross the end of a garden and join a lane. Cross straight over a road onto the road opposite **[NY500 628]**. At the next junction bear left and then, as the road turns left, continue straight ahead onto a path. Continue through the field on the right hand side of a fence. In the next field switch to walking on the left hand side of the fence. Continue through 4 fields in this direction and then pass through a kissing gate onto a green lane. The lane leads into the hamlet of Old Wall. Cross the road and continue straight ahead across the fields until you reach Bleatarn Farm. Cross the farm track and head across the middle of a small paddock.

Here you will find the Stall in the Wall, cold drinks and snacks and an honesty box.

3. Head across the middle of the next field and join a lane which leads to a road. Continue straight ahead along the road which has been built on top of the wall. Pass Low Wall Head farm on the left hand side before turning left down a track. The track becomes a grassy lane. At a plantation turn right onto another track. Follow this to the end and turn left to cross a bridge over the main road **[NY454

598].

High Crosby Farm on the left hand side has a wooden summer house with kettle, fridge, freezer and honesty box.

4. Carry straight on and turn right to walk along the road (The Roman Stanegate) into the village of Low Crosby. Pass the Stagg Inn on the right hand side. Turn left down a dead-end road and continue straight on along a track to reach the riverbank **[NY444 593]**. Turn right to follow the riverbank path. The well defined path continues and then turns right towards some trees. Continue parallel to the river as far as possible, then turn right alongside a hedge. Pass through a gate and turn left at a junction of tracks. Continue along the tree-lined track, signposted Linstock.

5. On entering a housing estate keep straight ahead along the road opposite. After the houses turn right onto a road and then left over the motorway **[NY423 579]**. Follow a lane which passes The Beeches, and you can then join a footpath which runs alongside the lane. Continue along until you cross a bridge and turn left along a tarmac path running through Rickerby Park. Cross the footbridge and turn right to follow the riverside path.

The path through Rickerby Park.

6. Shortly afterwards, at some railings, turn sharp left onto Catholic Lane [**NY408 563**]. Bear sharp right and continue straight on into Strand Road. Go under the subway and turn left onto Albert Street. Continue to the end and turn right onto Victoria Place. At the end turn left onto Lowther Street and follow this to the railway station at the end [**NY402 555**]. Jump onto a Virgin Pendolino to be wafted back to where you started walking 13 days ago!

APPENDIX

Ferguson Grading System (`FGS`)

1. Introduction

The FGS has been adopted as a means of assessing the nature and severity of the various walks in this book and the abilities and equipment needed to tackle each one safely. The FGS was developed by Stuart Ferguson, a long time fell and trail runner, climber, mountaineer, mountain-biker and general outdoor enthusiast. In the opinion of Trailguides the FGS is the most accurate and comprehensive grading system for comparing off-road walking, running and mountain-biking routes anywhere in the country.

2. The System

Tables 1 & 2, set out below, are used in order to give a grading to each route. Table 1 sets out three categories of country that a route could potentially cross, together with a range of factors that would need to be considered when tackling that route. The three categories are, Trail, Fell and Mountain, and after assessing which category best fits the route, a letter, either `T`, `F` or `M`, is allocated to that route. Where a route does not fit perfectly into one of the three categories the closest category is allocated.

Table 2 deals with five specific aspects of the route, distance, navigation, terrain, remoteness and height gain, and each one is allocated a letter, `D`, `N`, `T`, `R`, and `H`. Each letter is also given a severity score from the range 0-3 or 0-4, in respect of distance (`D`). The higher the number, the more severe the route. The five severity scores are then added together to give an overall score. The overall score is then put with the Table 1 category letter (i.e. `T`, `F` or `M`).

In order to show how the grading has been determined for each walk in this book, the five individual severity scores are set out, in square brackets, immediately after the actual grading. So, for example, Day 6 Hawes to Keld has a grading of F8 [D2, N1, T1, R2, H2], indicating that it is a Fell Category walk with a total severity score of 8. This is made up of the five specific severity scores, for distance (`D`), navigation (`N`), terrain (`T`), remoteness (`R`) and height gain (`H`), of 2, 1, 1, 2 and 2 respectively. The highest total severity score which can be achieved is 16 and the lowest total severity score achievable is 0.

The table which accompanies the grading with each walk sets out the specific factors, extracted from Table 2, that need to be considered when tackling that particular walk.

TABLE 1

	TRAIL	FELL	MOUNTAIN
Description	Lowland and forest areas including urban, cultivated and forested locations.	Moorlands and upland areas which may include some upland cultivated and forestry areas plus possibly remote locations.	Upland and mountain areas including remote and isolated locations.
Height	Not usually above 1,000 feet but may go up to 2,500 feet	Usually above 1,000 feet, up to 2,500 feet and above.	Usually above 2,500 feet and up to 4,000 feet.
Way-marking	Usually	Limited	None
Terrain	Usually graded paths, tracks and trails but may include some off-trail	May include some graded paths, tracks and trails but mainly off-trail	Virtually all off-trail
Height gain	Limited height gain	May include considerable height gain	May include some severe height gain.
Effects of weather	Very limited effect	May be prone to sudden weather changes	Extreme weather a possibility
Navigational skills	None to basic	Basic to competent	Competent to expert
Equipment	Walking shoes/boots. Possibly waterproofs Food and drink dependant upon route.	3/4 season walking boots. Full waterproof cover. Possibly map and compass dependant upon route. Food and drink dependant upon route.	Mountain boots. Full waterproof cover. Map and compass. Food and drink
Escape Routes	Yes	Some	Some to nil

TABLE 2

Score	0	1	2	3	4
Distance	Up to 6 miles	6 – 12 miles	12 – 18 miles	18 miles +	24 miles +
Navigation	No navigation skills needed	Basic navigation skills needed	Competent navigation skills needed	Expert navigation skills needed	
Terrain	75% + on graded track or path	50 – 75% on graded track or path 25 – 50% off track	25 -50% on graded track or path 50 – 75% off track	Under 25% on graded track or path Over 75% off track	
Remoteness	Urban	Countryside in fairly close proximity to habitation – at least 80% of the route within 2 miles	Countryside not in close proximity to habitation – less than 20% of the route within 2 miles	Remote, isolated location	
Height gain	Less than 100 ft per mile	Over 100 ft per mile	Over 125 ft per mile	Over 250 ft per mile	

Notes to Table 2

Graded paths = Well established paths with a stable surface.
Escape routes = The opportunity to cut the route short and return to the start without completing the full course in the event of weather changes or unforeseen incidents.

The Author

Steve Garrill

Steve is a teacher at Saint Bede's Catholic High School in Lytham St Annes. He is also a Duke of Edinburgh assessor and every year organises a team to take the Yorkshire 3 Peaks Challenge to raise money for charity. Steve took up long distance walking in his early 40's and since then has completed most of the long distance walks in the north of England and Scotland. With his experience he has learnt the value of careful preparation, advanced planning and having the right equipment.

He trained as a history teacher and is interested in the history of every walk he undertakes. This walk has a strong link with Roman history, but there are interesting links with many other periods of history throughout the walk. Steve has given brief outlines of historical connections and added reliable website addresses where further information can be obtained.

Steve is keen to promote walking for all of its many benefits, but equally keen that people are not put off when their early experiences are ruined by inadequate preparation, poor equipment or misleading directions. Every section of this walk has been walked twice, three or even four times to check the accuracy of the directions given.

Trailguides Limited

Trailguides is a small independent publisher specialising in publications for those who enjoy the great outdoors. Our target is to produce guides that are as user-friendly and informative as possible and all in an easily readable format. In essence to increase the enjoyment of the user and to showcase the very best of the great British countryside. Our series of books explores the heritage of us all and lets you see our landscape with new eyes. These books are written to not just take you on a walk but to investigate, explore and understand the objects, places and history that has shaped not just the land but also the people of this country.

If you've enjoyed following the routes in this guide and want news and details of other publications that are being developed by Trailguides then look at the company website at **www.trailguides.co.uk**

Comments and, yes, criticisms, are always welcomed especially if you discover a change to a route. Contact us by email through the website or by post at Trailguides Limited, 35 Carmel Road South, Darlington, Co Durham DL3 8DQ.

Other walking books from Trailguides.
At the time of publication the following books are also available but with new titles being regularly added to our publication list keep checking our website.

County Durham.
Hamsterley Forest.
The Barningham Trail.
Ancient Stones.
The High Hills of Teesdale.
Walks from Stanhope.
Mid-Teesdale Walks.
Walking in Weardale.

East Sussex.
Walks in 1066 Country.
The 1066 Country Walk.

Northumberland.
The Cheviot Hills.
Walks from Wooler.
The Hills of Upper Coquetdale.
Walks from Kirknewton.
Walks Around Rothbury and Coquetdale.
Walks on the Wild Side: The Cheviot Hills
Walks in Hadrian's Wall Country.

North Yorkshire.
Walking the Hills of Upper Swaledale.
Walks around Gunnerside.
Walking around Reeth & Upper Swaledale.
Walking around Osmotherley and the Cleveland Hills.

Walking North East.
Visit our website and sign up to receive our free newsletter, Walking North East, dedicated to walking in North Eastern England. Full of news, views and articles relating to this the forgotten corner of England.

Disclaimer

The information contained in these pages and the route descriptions is provided in good faith, but no warranty is made for its accuracy. The contents are, at the time of writing and to the best of our knowledge, up-to-date and correct. However, the world is a changing environment and what is correct one day may not be so the next. Care should always be taken when following these route descriptions just as it should when following maps or waymarkers of any kind..

No guarantee whatsoever is provided by the author and/or Trailguides Limited and no liability is accepted for any loss, damage or injury of any kind resulting from the use of this book, nor as a result of any defect or inaccuracy in it.

As with all outdoor activities, you and you alone are responsible for your safety and well being.